Robert H. Schuller

Success is Never Ending

Failure is Never Final

THOMAS NELSON PUBLISHERS
Nashville

Published in Nashville, Tennessee, by Thomas Nelson, Inc., and distributed in Canada by Lawson Falle, Ltd., Cambridge, Ontario.

Scripture quotations are from THE NEW KING JAMES VERSION of the Bible. Copyright © 1979, 1980, 1982 Thomas Nelson, Inc., Publishers.

Printed in the United States of America.
ISBN 0-8407-5529-5

*To my wife, the one single person who—
more than any other human—has not only
made my success possible but also brought
honor and nobility to the whole process:*

This book is dedicated to you

—Arvella—

with all my love.

ACKNOWLEDGMENTS

Many thanks to the several contributors whose stories appear in these pages to inspire and challenge us. A special word of thanks to my chief researcher and editor, Sheila Coleman. Then to my wife, Arvella, who patiently worked through each sentence and made many invaluable contributions. To both of you—thanks and God bless you.

PART I Success is Never Ending...

contents

PART II ...*Failure is Never Final!*

Success
is Never
Ending . . .

CHAPTER 1

Success
or Failure

The Choice
Is Yours!

*T*wenty years ago I developed a philosophy for successful living that I called "Possibility Thinking."

Today I look back and rejoice over the success of this system.

Wow! Has it worked for me! And I know it can work for you!

In the past two decades my family has grown to include five fantastic children—all very successful—and ten grand-children—all potentially great Possibility Thinkers! And my career in ministry has been (and continues to be) rewarding, exciting, and challenging!

Yes, this success system called Possibility Thinking works wonders for those who practice it. I've seen thousands of persons who have achieved incredible goals and overcome amazing obstacles and handicaps with the help of Possibility Thinking! Consider these results:

  • As a young boy in our church, David Leestma used to say, "I want to be an astronaut when I grow up."

Well, his parents, Reverend and Mrs. Harold Leestma, ministers on my staff, really encouraged this positive attitude. David graduated at the top of his class at the U.S. Naval Academy in Annapolis and went on to make his dream come true. He became an astronaut and walked in space!

- They dreamed of becoming major league ball players—they made their dreams come true! Bert Blyleven and Lenny Dykstra learned Possibility Thinking in my church. And they have both played in the Fall Classic—and *won*!

- Nearly two million letters come across my desk each year from people telling me how Possibility Thinking "saved their life!" They heard me preach it on T.V. They tried it—and are living proof it works!

I could fill this book with other success stories of people who became Possibility Thinkers and incredible achievers. They have succeeded in all walks of life in society, in business, in education, in industry, in government, in the military. Possibility Thinking worked for them. It can work for you. You, too, can be a success!

It all begins when you decide you want to succeed. Some people, frankly, run from success. They are embarrassed by the subject. After all, "success" has taken a lot of criticism—much of it undeserved—some deserved.

If success is achieved through exploitation of the poor or the oppressed, then such injustice is sinful. When it is necessary to succeed in order to feed insatiable greed, such success deserves to be rebuked!

A world renowned movie producer and director invited a very good friend of mine to accompany him to a bank in Geneva, Switzerland. My friend went with him into a private bank vault. Inside were piles and piles of solid gold bars! Tens of millions of dollars!

My friend described the scene: "With gleaming eyes, the movie director said to me, 'Isn't that the most beautiful sight you ever saw!' I looked at him and I almost became ill. In that moment he radiated a spirit of all-consuming greed, and it made his countenance ugly, repulsive, repugnant!"

Such an image of success deserves to be condemned.

By contrast I have a friend named Armand Hammer, a super Possibility Thinker! You can read his book.[1] He was a millionaire at age twenty-one and is an enormously successful and wealthy man. However, he has shared his money with the impoverished and used it to underwrite the research and development of projects that will help mankind. Only God knows how many causes, projects, institutions, and individuals have been financially helped by this wonderful philanthropist! This is the kind of success this book salutes!

Likewise, consider the success of my friend the late Foster McGaw. When he was still a young salesman, he discovered that hospitals did not purchase their own equipment. In many cases doctors sent nurses out to drugstores to pick up bandages.

He hit upon a wonderful idea: to call regularly in the hospitals and provide them with the supplies that they would need. His offer to help was accepted by doctors and hospitals alike.

He promptly went to the manufacturers and became a supplier to the nation's hospitals. So the American Hospital Supply Corporation was born.

Foster McGaw lived to give away more than $150 million in gifts. Over thirty colleges received gifts of $1 million or more. Our Crystal Cathedral received two such gifts! Real success is really exciting!

Success to another friend, George Petty, meant creating jobs to save the life of an entire town!

"I have a speaking engagement you have to accept, Dr. Schuller," George said one day in a strong and determined voice. "I want you to dedicate my new plant in Wisconsin. After all, our success is due to your Possibility Thinking."

He went on to explain, "I was reading in the *Wall Street Journal* that the entire town of Kimberly, Wisconsin, was doomed to become a ghost town. The town had been built around a paper-making plant seventy-five years before. It

---

[1]Armand Hammer and Neil Lyndon, *Hammer: A Witness to History* (New York: Putnam, 1987).

was the only industry that really created jobs in this town. But modern times made the factory nonprofitable. I read this sad story, and the next morning I heard you, Dr. Schuller, espouse your Possibility Thinking on television. You said, 'Nobody has a money problem—it's always an idea problem.' So I called in one of my top executives and said, 'Will you tell me what it would take to produce paper at a profit in that town?'

"Some days later my associate handed me a note. The news was devastating! His plan required a new machine that could turn out coated paper 223 inches wide—and ⅔ of a mile long—every minute! The machine could be built, *but* it would be nearly 500 feet long and would cost more than $50 million! And if market conditions were right and financing were reasonable, it could prove profitable!"

George Petty dedicated himself then and there to "go for it!" He went to manufacturers and government officials in his native country, Canada, and asked, "Would you like the business of building the key machinery components? Will you finance the manufacturing costs?" They agreed to do so.

Next, he went to the largest magazines in the world. "Would you like to be guaranteed the delivery of all the paper you need and not be 'caught short' a few years from now? If so, advance me cash, and I'll guarantee you future delivery." They did.

And so George Petty put the "impossible deal" together! Then he called me. "Dr. Schuller—the machine is ready to be started up. We're dedicating it next month. We have saved the town of Kimberly, Wisconsin! And we have actually added six hundred new jobs! You'll have to come out for the grand opening and celebration."

I did. I'll never forget it! Flags of the United States and Canada flew from every light pole in town. There was a parade complete with music by the high school band, pom poms, and "On, Wisconsin!" There was a huge tent to house nearly a thousand VIPs flown in on private jets from New York and Canada!

George Petty had put everything he had and owned on the line! Thousands would benefit from his personally *risky* venture. Although, it nearly did him in when prime interest rates rose two years later to an unimaginable 22 percent, he made it! He struggled through and succeeded!

Success—let's not knock it; let's not block it; let's UN-LOCK it! But first let's understand what success/failure is all about.

Success/Failure: *Is it more than winning and losing?* Yes. Because success is a process. It's more than what you read on the scoreboard. Success and failure don't stop when the game ends and the crowd goes home. We have all seen winners whose success turned them into swollen-headed "jerks." Their victory was their downfall. And we have all seen losers who were such great sports and took their losses so graciously that they turned their defeat into a personal victory.

Success/Failure: *Is it about setting goals and striving to reach them?* Yes. But it's more than what you will read in the final report or the published news release. For real success is *accepting* your God-given opportunities and *giving* your divinely-inspired goals 110 percent of your best effort!

Success may actually elude you until that moment when you fail. The pole vaulter's efforts are not complete nor does he win until he fails to clear the highest hurdle! In failing, the pole vaulter arrives at success!

Success is discovering and developing your potential as well as seeing the new opportunities born all around you every new day!

Success/Failure: *Is it about solving problems and resolving difficulties?* Yes. But understand success is a process that must never stop. So you've solved one problem? This success will spawn new problems! You've resolved one difficulty? This success will hatch a batch of new ones. So real success will finally be measured by how charming, graceful, polite, and positive you have become through this evolving process.

Success/Failure: *Is it about acquiring fame and fortune?* Yes—and no. Again and again makers and shakers of wealth and power have been some of the world's greatest human beings, while others have been the crown punks of history! Fame and fortune are shallow goals unless they are a means to an end, a way to help others.

I hope that success will mean prosperity for you. For the alternative to prosperity could be poverty. And poverty becomes terribly oppressive. How many people in the poverty pockets of our world have opted for dictatorships because they lacked the hope of financial independence? Desperate, hungry, poor people have been tempted to trade their freedom for bread. Poverty leaves depressed, discouraged, and defeated people at the mercy of any dictator who comes along with promises (solid or hollow) that hold out hope! We spread freedom from oppression as we move people from the poverty to the prosperity column. As more and more citizens become financially independent and as the conditions that spawn and sustain dictatorships are wiped out, democracy is made more secure. Persons who believe that they can achieve financial independence will be slow to buy the false promises of self-serving, power-hungry politicians who manipulate and exploit the poor with the promise of a larger handout.

SO, WHAT THEN IS SUCCESS?

Success for the husband and wife means making their marriage work with the hope that they can celebrate a golden wedding anniversary! Success will mean keeping their family intact with communication lines open so this community of caring and sharing persons will enjoy each other in love.

Success for the student means passing the courses in school and developing mind and talents to make a beneficial contribution to the human race!

Success for the surgeon means saving a life!

Success for the lawyer means helping confused persons extricate themselves from the tangled webs of conflicting involvements, setting them free again.

Success for the teacher means motivating students to believe that they are smart—not stupid—and helping students develop self-images that will lift them to heights they never before dreamed!

Success for the salesperson means discovering people who have problems that will probably be solved by the salesperson's product or service.

Success for the law enforcement officials and those in our military services means maintaining peace and order.

Success for the pastor of the local church means administering programs to serve the spiritual needs of the church family. It means effectively communicating the hope of the gospel to people who have no faith.

Success for the people who are ill means restored health or, at the very least, handling the illness in such a way that they inspire others around them.

Success can mean coping with unusual problems. For instance, for my daughter who lost her leg in a motorcycle accident, success today means carrying her precious little baby girl while walking on an artificial leg. As she was walking out her front door, with her husband at her side, the unthinkable happened—she lost her balance on the sidewalk, and though saving herself from a fall, she watched her eight-week-old, curly-haired baby girl fly out of her arms, through the air, and onto the lawn—narrowly missing the sidewalk.

The next night my wife was at Carol's home. It happened again to the horror of my wife and our twenty-three-year-old daughter! This time Carol and her baby fell on the carpeted floor. As I put this book to press, my daughter is still dealing with this challenge. So success for her will mean being able to carry her nursing Rebekah and never drop her again!

Success can mean acquiring more money or material things. Surely our perception of success should not ignore the material needs of life. As Christians we're not opposed to material success if it means that people will be able to (a) provide for the development of their own potential education, (b) enjoy health care, or (c) start a business that could provide an outlet for their creative skills in the creation or distribution of a product or service, and (d) enable them to experience the "joy of giving" to great movements, causes, ministries, and institutions in this world of hunger and pain.

As I was growing up my family was poor, but every Sunday we were able to drop some money in the offering plate. As long as you can afford to *give* a dollar to some beautiful charity, you will never really feel poor! You will feel rich. That's why *I've always felt wealthy!*

Success may or may not mean that you've acquired a lot. It does mean that you have become a generous person.

Few restaurateurs are more successful than Keo Sananikone, in Honolulu, Hawaii. A refugee from Laos, Keo took a night job washing dishes and working in the kitchen at Pizza Hut. "I did not have enough experience to open my own restaurant," he said. During the day he worked as a bilingual math teacher at McKinley High School.

In 1977, with an investment of about $26,000, Keo opened his first restaurant—Mekong. Despite the tiny size and the lack of a liquor license, Mekong quickly became popular because of the outstanding food, remarkably low prices, and excellent service. "Even though Mekong was a hole-in-the-wall, I tried to create a pleasant atmosphere with dim lights. That's the way I like it when I go out to dine," said Keo.

"There were no employees, just family working," Keo recalled. "All of us worked at other jobs. We switched off so that the ones with day jobs worked dinner and ones with night jobs worked lunch."

After eight months, Keo hired his first two employees. Ten years later he has 142 employees at his four restaurants and a waiting list of about 300 applicants who would love to work at one of the popular Thai restaurants.

"I love to work with people and I love to entertain," Keo said. "I feel like I'm hosting a party every night. I always knew I would be successful. Not successful in the sense of how much I accumulate, but I am happy and I laugh a lot. That is success to me. A lady once asked me, 'How does it feel to be successful and have a lot of money now?' I told her, 'Success has nothing to do with money.' I feel I was successful because I had a good education, good friends, and I was happy all around."

So what does success finally add up to? A diploma on

the wall? A trophy in the case? Money in the bank? Professional honors? Yes, this is success, but more than this, success is being able to look at yourself in the mirror and be proud of the person you have become! You did the best you could!

Success is noblest when it leaves you with the self-respect that you have been a good steward of the life, liberties, possibilities, and opportunities that God offered to you.

Success is building your own self-respect by affirming the dignity of your fellow human beings. This is why some of the most successful persons I've known were (and are) among the most beloved and respected people on earth even though their material acquisitions were modest. They're Great Hearts! They're Super Souls! They're Precious Persons! They are the *really* beautiful people—fashion, fortune, lifestyle notwithstanding. Number my farmer father in that honored Hall of Fame of Great Human Beings! He struggled. He prevailed over immense challenges. His neighbors and relatives admired, respected, and loved him. And Dad respected himself too!

That is success!

Yes, Dad bought and paid for his farm. It fed him until he died. Was that the end of his successful life? Hardly. His children inherited a portion. I took my share and bought a piece of real estate. Years later, the land had greatly increased in value. When we were raising money to build the Crystal Cathedral, I gave that investment to help pay for a chunk of the Cathedral, where it shelters and houses persons who come and are transformed. My father's success goes on and on and on.

So!

Success is never ending
because success is a process!

You, too, will never be able to measure all the good you do! It will trickle down and ripple on! And on!

Consider the persons whose success is defined in the arena of self-improvement. To confront a raw reality honestly, without denial, is real success. Illustration: The alcoholic who stops denying his condition, goes to Alcoholics Anonymous, and becomes sober. He is a success!

"But he started drinking again," the cynic complains. So? Has his *success* ended? No! Those weeks, months, years while he was sober—weren't they wonderful? Something great happened during that winning streak! Positive memories were generated and collected and will remain *permanently recorded* in the person's mind and in the memories of others inspired by that streak of successful sobriety. *Who can measure the long-range redemptive impact of a single inspiring memory?*

While the alcoholic was sober, his testimony inspired others to take life-changing steps. Some of them are still sober today! And they're inspiring others who will inspire others. So even if the alcoholic "falls off the program," the past successes, however brief, ripple on in other lives!

Meanwhile, the memory of the winning streak will, more often than not, at the right time overpower the shame of "falling off the wagon." And this alcoholic whose success streak supposedly ended will come back again! Inspiring flashbacks of positive memories will become replays in slow motion, drawing the person back to another AA meeting and he will be on his way again!

Really, his success is unstoppable! His success *stumbles but never stops!*

Success is never ending—even if you do add pounds after a successful diet! I recall a woman who came to me for counseling. She finally faced the fact that she was fat. She had been gaining weight but had tried for years to deny the reality of her condition. Then came the moment of truth! She saw herself as she really was (fat!) and had a sudden vision of the beautiful person she could become (slim!). So she joined a responsible weight loss program and lost ninety pounds! What a success!

Two years later she gained thirty pounds back. But once more she went on a diet—and lost—only to regain the poundage. Over a fifteen-year period she'd lose, then gain again. Finally, depressed, she was ready to give up and said to me, "I wasted all those battles."

"Not really," I said. "Count all the pounds you lost in all of the diets put together. Add that number to your present weight and tell me how heavy you'd be today."

She thought. A shocked look appeared on her face. "Gosh, I'd be over four hundred pounds!" she said. "I have had some success after all!"

"Of course," I answered, "you have had many successes! And every pound lost is a pound off your present weight today."

Success is never ending—even if the marriage doesn't last forever! They were so starry-eyed at their wedding. The first few months were great! Then came the storm. Rocks seemed to lie just beneath the surface waiting to emerge with the changing tide. I counseled with them. Then their fragile craft struck a barely-hidden rock. That did it. All efforts to save the marriage couldn't keep them from the divorce courts. But divorce couldn't kill the attraction that kept drawing them together. They tried again! "Would you remarry us, Dr. Schuller?" *At this point we defined success as reconciliation!*

The couple was willing to cancel an agreement they had their first time around—an agreement never to have children. Ten months after their remarriage their daughter was born. The baptism was precious. They were succeeding after all. Right? Yes! But ten years later the marriage unraveled again. This time the husband was sexually involved with another woman, and no one could stop him from abandoning his wife and daughter. This time the divorce was final.

One negative thinker said to me, "It's too bad they had a child! It would be so much easier for both of them if they hadn't!"

"How shortsighted that perception is," I protested. "Their successful streak of marriage can never, ever, really end!" I was more prophetic than I realized! Today, twenty-two years later, I have seen the "little girl I baptized" become a university graduate and a beautiful kindergarten teacher!

Success, however short-running, quickly drops seeds that will find refuge in some likely or unlikely spot to grow, thrive, and reproduce. When will success stop? Never! It goes on! And on! And on!

I lived closely through the "rise and fall" of Richard Nixon's presidency. He was, after all, a neighbor in Orange County, California. No president had ever before resigned the office. His term was a disgrace. A total failure! Yet history will record that President Nixon built the bridge between China and America. No serious critic can underestimate the immense success of this stroke of international diplomacy. So, ironically, the success process of this dethroned president goes on! Success is never ending!

So this is success—to do something good, when you can, where you can, while you can! If, down the road, a tragic collision "ends it all," remember, *nothing can ever really end it all!*

Does success stop when you sin and stumble? Or have you left seeds behind that will sprout and bear fruit? Religious history will long remember the sad, deplorable, dishonorable disgrace in the 1980s of a television ministry known as "PTL," founded by Jim and Tammy Bakker. The confessed sins and foibles of this pair created an opportunity for cynics and non-Christians to cast despicable judgment against all religious television ministries—my own included. I cannot imagine ever having to live through a more painful year in public ministry. The damage done to respectable Christians by the Bakker episode is impossible to measure! So this "PTL success" came to a screeching, scorching, searing, seamy end. Really? In a public auction of the extravagant properties purchased by the Bakkers, one couple appeared on television to explain why they bought Tammy Bakker's desk. "We were both saved by their ministry," they said. "Nothing can change that. We never want to stop being thankful for the good they brought to our lives, and probably a million others. They led us to the Lord Jesus Christ and Jesus hasn't let us down." So even here, success is never ending—and failure is never final.

One of California's most successful home builders fell

upon bad times. The real estate market plummeted. He was left holding the bag. The upshot was bankruptcy. He had built over 10,000 single-family residences on the California coast. But now he was out of business. It was my job as his pastor to lift him from the black and bleak despair of this failure.

"You haven't stopped succeeding just because you're going into bankruptcy," I told him. "You have been forced into bankruptcy because your accounts receivable have lost their value. But look at the homes you have built! They're still standing. Look at the salary checks you have paid out to subcontractors and laborers over the past twenty years! That money is still providing underpinnings for institutions and businesses that you'll never know about! No small amount of that money you paid out over the past twenty years is in private savings accounts today. Some of it will be used to send a child through college twenty years from now! Doctors, teachers, and leaders in society will be educated from savings made possible by paychecks you issued!"

I continued, "How much of the money you paid in salaries ended up in retirement funds to be drawn out of pensions ten, twenty, thirty years from today? Your business has come to an end. That's true. But your success keeps going on and on and on! How much of the money you paid was invested in stock and real estate, which will be inherited by children and their children's children? Just because your corporation is bankrupt doesn't mean your success has come to an end! The process of success continues to live—changing shape in changing lives!"

Likewise, a pastor once saw his little congregation dwindle until the doors of the church were closed. The property was sold. The life of a local congregation came to an end. He was terribly depressed. "But your successes have not stopped!" I told him. "Just because the church doors are bolted and the property is sold does not mean there aren't children of members of this church who are enjoying better lives because of the Christian values they have received. There are immortal souls who will enjoy everlasting life in heaven! Nothing can stop that! Consider the good you and your fellow members have done by encouraging each other and helping struggling and grief-stricken souls through their lonely and lost and painful crises in life!"

Success is never ending because success is like the process of seed planting. Good deeds, honestly offered, immediately are transformed into fertile seeds. Every creative, redemptive contribution, like a seed planted, *will bear fruit!* And only God can count the apples in a seed. The farm can go broke or be sold to a developer, but the land won't evaporate! It will remain as a base of productivity for someone! Meanwhile, a stream of human beings were kept alive, for a season, by food from that farm. And while they were kept alive, they made love and bore children, and so the fruit of the seed goes on and on and on!

Think of this: You and I owe our lives to successful people we'll never be able to thank personally:

• Consider the freedom we enjoy! Some soldier died for that! His success goes on! Thank you, Sir!

• Some medical researcher wiped out a disease years ago. Thank you, Madame!

• Some believers held on to the Christian faith through seasons of persecution! Their success is never ending! Thank you!

So I say to all good people on planet Earth: *Your greatest successes will forever remain God's secret.* Only He will know how much good we have all done. A little good helps a lot more than we will ever know, for that person who has been helped will help somebody else. The death of a caterpillar and birth of a butterfly do not mean that the caterpillar has stopped succeeding. There is, in all of life, the universal principle of death and resurrection. Life goes on. And on. And on!

Even apparent failures can become important ingredients in the process of success! Suppose the doctor does his best but the patient dies. Does this mean the doctor has failed? Not completely! The doctor has succeeded on the *research level,* for something has been learned—what does not work. Failures then become significant contributions to the process of future success—perhaps the cure for some form of cancer or another serious disease.

This positive perception of failure is all-important! Without it, enthusiasm disappears. Depression moves in. Discouragement takes over. Energy dries up. Resources no longer supply life to the enterprise.

If that is what success is all about, then what is real failure? Real failure is:

- Failing personally, not professionally!
- Yielding to cowardice in the face of an urgent but risky venture!
- Retreating from a high calling to a noble duty because you fear imperfection in the execution of that duty.
- Protecting your pride from a possibly embarrassing professional failure rather than promoting a wonderful and worthy cause.
- Demoting faith from the leadership of your life and promoting fear to a position of power.

This is real failure as a person. But here's the good news: If you are, or have ever been, a failure, it never needs to be final! You can reverse your fortune and your future by changing your thinking!

Yes, I promise you that in this book you too can find (a) the motivation to succeed and (b) the management skills to succeed! You'll discover that success is the process of managing your greatest asset—YOU! In this book—

- You'll be inspired to dream a new dream!
- You'll be encouraged to try to succeed!
- You'll become a Possibility Thinker and believe that nothing is impossible!

Yes, this is success: To dare to dream the impossible dream with God and to give God a chance to make this dream come true!

Isn't success fantastic? YES! And it's yours to choose!

Choose it! Seek it! For success is finding a need and filling it! Finding a hurt and healing it! Finding a problem and solving it!

All the while we must remember that *there is no success*

without sacrifice. Jesus said, "He who loses his life for My sake will find it" (Matt. 10:39). Satisfying success will never really come to the self-serving person! Rather it is the sincere, self-sacrificing spirit that inspires, sustains, and sanctifies success.

I know a young man who died in his early thirties after a brief public career brought him fame in his time and in his territory. The tragic element in his life story is that after stunning success he was falsely accused of a crime that resulted in his imprisonment, trial, and execution! The death penalty was carried out. The end of his life was utter disgrace, humiliation, and shame. I could weep as I think of the whole sad, sordid spectacle of this social injustice. I doubt if there is another case in history where a bright mind and a good heart rose so rapidly to prominence and popularity only to drop so precipitously in the public eye!

So success does end—doesn't it? He failed—didn't he? Not really! His comeback was solid—and sensational! So his perceived failure was not final! That young man's name was eventually vindicated. His honor was restored by honest and honorable followers. His name today is the most respected and renowned name in the world. He's my friend! My inspiration! His name is Jesus Christ.

Check out His character, His career, His triumph over adversity and death, and you'll agree: Success is never ending and failure is never final.

CHAPTER 2

Dream Your Way to Unending Success!

So now you know! This book is about—
- Success and Failure,
- Exasperation and Inspiration,
- Frustration and Fulfillment,
- Discouragement and Hope!

This book is for you! And it is about how to make your dreams come true!

When I meet people they greet me with the usual question, "Hello, Dr. Schuller—how are you?"

"Great." I pause, smile, and add, "I plan it that way! For success doesn't just happen! You have to *plan* to *make* it happen!"

I learned that when I was a little boy. I was approaching my fifth birthday when my mother's brother, a Princeton graduate serving as a missionary in China, returned to America on furlough. We had been awaiting his arrival for months. At our simple country table, Uncle Henry was idolized: he was George Washington; he was Abraham Lincoln;

he was Theodore Roosevelt. He was a hero of epic proportions.

My mother was close to her younger scholar-statesman brother. She was proud of Uncle Henry. He had gone from a farm in Iowa to postgraduate studies in theology at Princeton and then—in the 1920s—to that mystic, mysterious, marvelous country on the other side of our earth! Carefully he and his bride had packed their limited possessions in a large steamer trunk and planned their trip by train to California. There they would board a steamer, and weeks later they would arrive in China—busy and bustling—struggling, suffering, and striving China—land of people in black clothes, pointed straw hats, and sandals!

Uncle Henry was a dreamer—and a doer! He was an achiever! He was a planner and a producer! He thought big! He talked big! He delivered big! So people believed him; he was listened to. He was a leader who knew what he wanted to do and where he wanted to go.

Uncle Henry had sent postcards year after year. I had looked at these strange photographs, so foreign to my small world of an Iowa farmhouse, barn, chicken house, hog house, corncrib—an isolated settlement at the dead end of a lonely road. No wonder I was excited at Uncle Henry's homecoming.

"He'll be here in an hour," Mom said. "Harold, go get some fresh water." (She always called me by my middle name. It was her favorite name. Robert had been her strong-willed mother's choice. So I was named Robert Harold. Grandma had her way! But so did my mother. She simply ignored my first name, and Grandma was satisfied.)

With a small pail, I walked across the open farmyard to the pump that was twice as tall as I. Silhouetted in the flat open space it appeared to be an iron creature with a body and a life of its own: the handle an arm, the spout its head. After a few vigorous up and down pushes of the handle, the water came spurting out—clean, clear, cold! The well was our family's friend! Now it would give us the fresh drink we could offer our honored guest!

As I walked toward the house, bearing the best beverage

I had ever tasted, I looked down the long, lonely, one-lane, dry, dusty farm road. Off in the distance, just this side of the horizon, I saw a small cloud of dust that grew larger—and longer—coming toward our place! Then I saw a black car emerge from the dust.

"He's coming, Momma! He's here!" I shouted. I ran—spilling water—up the splintering, unpainted, wooden steps, and through the screen door, across the faded and cracked linoleum kitchen floor.

"Uncle Henry's come!" I shouted to Momma, who (it seemed to me) was always in the kitchen, morning, noon, night.

I ran back outdoors. A small lawn composed of an odd mixture of wild grasses surrounded our small, two-story, white farmhouse. A simple fence kept out a horse or cow that might get loose. My bare feet skipped across the broken cement sidewalk where weeds grew through cracks that were also portals to vast underground chambers where millions of ants lived and worked.

Now I was at the gate—to wait. I could hear the car! It was Grandpa's new black 1926 Chevrolet. *Everybody* in the small world I knew drove Chevys or Fords. And at family gatherings adults would heatedly argue as to which car was better.

Now Grandpa was proudly chauffeuring his oldest son, Henry! Sophisticated! Elite! World traveler! A man with a mission! The car stopped. Clouds of dust swirled around the four-door sedan. I nervously fingered my Oshkosh overalls. In the pockets I kept my only earthly possessions . . . a few precious marbles made of glass! To me they were diamonds! Emeralds! Jewels!

The car door opened (so did my eyes)! I was about to meet the person who was my superstar! Top celebrity! Sensational success! He was, in my time and my world, Michael Jackson! Lionel Richie! Mohammed Ali! Bob Hope! Frank Sinatra! Ronald Reagan! Magic Johnson! To that boy, four years and eleven months old, Uncle Henry was the most important person alive on planet Earth.

I would be the first member of my family to see him! I

was ahead of my brother and sister, who were still at school. He was handsome. He wore a suit! A white shirt! A tie! He was all dressed up like, I supposed, a well-educated person should be. He was energetic. I was awestruck! He bounded up to me.

Staring at my flesh-and-blood hero, I was speechless, breathless. Then out came his booming voice. "So you're Robert. Yes! You must be Robert Harold."

I nodded my head. I waited.

"You, Robert—" he said. (His hand was on my head! He was looking at me, his eyes close to mine! I was the only living person he knew at that moment! Then he spoke! Strong! Clear! A pronouncement! A prediction! An affirmation! A prophecy!) "You, Robert, will be a minister when you grow up."

That was all it took. Those few seconds changed my destiny; they determined my course in life. I stood staring after him, clutching my dream to my heart as Uncle Henry bounded into the arms of his sister.

I was deeply, permanently impressed. He had given me a gift of far greater value than the "diamonds and emeralds" in my denim pockets: Uncle Henry had come all the way from China with the greatest gift I would ever receive from anyone—a dream! A fantastic possibility! I knew beyond a shadow of a doubt what I would become. After all, Uncle Henry had said it!

That night I prayed my daily childhood prayer: "Now I lay me down to sleep. I pray the Lord my soul to keep. If I should die before I wake, I pray the Lord, my soul to take." Then I added this new line—"And make me a preacher when I grow up. Amen."

At breakfast the next morning I announced my dream to my parents. I wondered why Dad cried.

How did my success happen? Why did my dreams come true? Does it matter? Of course! Does it make a difference? You bet! For whom? Only God knows. It certainly mattered and made a difference in my marriage, in my family—and in the lives of the people who were (and are) touched positively, redemptively, creatively by my life's efforts and achievements.

So I celebrate success today! What do I know about it? How did it happen? What have I learned that I can pass on to you?

I have learned that some people seem to "fall into" success. Originally it was not their intention, goal, or dream. Circumstances almost forced success upon them. However, their number (proportionately) is small. And there is little we can learn from them.

More importantly the vast majority of high achievers made it because they wanted to! A passionate desire to achieve was a consuming drive in their life. Check them out—I have! They use phrases like, "my dream," "my burning desire," "my consuming passion," "my overriding goal," "my sense of destiny."

I understand those people! I can relate to them! For I am one of them! You (no matter who you are) can learn from them! And I will joyously share with you what I have learned from sixty years of successful living. Here then—under solemn oath to the God I believe in—is my witness to the world on how my dreams came true! And continue to come true! Beautifully! Naturally! Nobly! Joyously! Like a flower emerging from seed, evolving from stem, unfolding from bud!

Here's How Dreams Come True!

"You and I deserve to be together today!" I announced to the audience. It was my opening line. There was a lump in my throat. A tear in my eye. Why? Because I was fulfilling one of the most honored invitations that had ever come to me.

It was the second time in ten years that I had been invited to give the baccalaureate address to the graduates of the United States Air Force Academy in Colorado Springs. The spectacular chapel was packed with proud relatives of the cadets.

The graduating class had come from fifty states, from

rich and powerful families as well as from the very poor. In more than one case a bright young boy or girl from an impoverished home had caught the attention of a U.S. senator. A college education would have been out of reach if the senator hadn't nominated them. But he had! They were accepted by the Air Force Academy! With the acceptance came a chance to receive a four-year, all-expense-paid college education of the highest caliber while earning a small salary.

But the work was hard. The hours of studying and training were arduous. And now, four years later, they were graduating! Standing tall and proud in crisp uniforms, they experienced the proudest moment of their lives! The incredible and impossible dream had come true!

A great pipe organ filled the chapel with martial music. The choir sang with resounding enthusiasm. Then it was time for me, the minister, to deliver the baccalaureate address. I looked across the audience and continued, explaining my opening declaration. "Yes! We belong together! For you and I—we are people who believe that *dreams do come true!*"

Then I briefly shared my own story of how my dreams had come true. "Fifty-five years ago when I was a little boy, my Uncle Henry gave me a dream—to become a minister and share the inspiring story of Jesus Christ with people. My family was poor but we didn't know it. We often put cardboard in our shoes when the leather soles wore through, leaving a hole the size of a nickel that exposed our feet to the dirt, gravel, and cement.

"A penny in my hand gave me a thrill almost equal to the thrill of a hundred-dollar bill today! We didn't have to worry about having enough to eat. We had a garden and lived off the land. But the prospect of years and years of expensive education was another matter." *(I could see my audience relating to that!)*

Continuing, I said, "I became a dreamer when I was barely five years old, hearing the call from Uncle Henry—actually from God Himself—to devote my life to the ministry.

"Even though the cost of education loomed impossibly

before me, my dream propelled me through high school and four years of college. I picked up odd jobs, worked through the summer and saved dollars, and earned my meals by working in the college cafeteria. Somehow everything worked out until, before I realized it, I graduated with my college degree, just as you cadets are graduating today! Yes, my college degree was a successful mountain peak in my life—as it is for you. We know that dreams come true!

"It took me three years after college to complete my postgraduate work in theology. Then I received my theological credentials and was qualified to be ordained and licensed as a minister in the Reformed Church in America. For that event my father returned to Holland, Michigan, the same town where earlier I had received my undergraduate degree. As I walked across the stage to receive my final formal educational credential, I noticed my father in the audience drying tears from his eyes.

"I remembered then how my father had cried that morning when I announced—at the tender age of nearly five— that I was going to be a minister. Now on the evening of my graduation from seminary my father shared his long and well-kept secret. I learned the truth behind the tears.

"'When I was a little boy I wanted to be a minister too,' he said to me. 'But my father and mother died, leaving me an orphan. I had to drop out of school after learning only how to read and write. I was forced to take the only job I could get—helping an Iowa farmer do his chores. At that point I watched my dream of becoming a minister fade away like a beautiful cloud that I watched grow larger and take shape— only to disappear! I prayed about it. And I asked God to let my dream come true through a son that I hoped He would give to me. Then my dream would not die. It could come true, through YOU!'

"At that point he looked at me, weeping, and said, 'I never dared to tell you this, Robert, because I didn't want you to become a minister just to please me. It had to be God Himself working in you, answering my prayer, or it wouldn't have been right!'

"He spoke firmly and passionately, 'That's why I never

told you why I was so thrilled when you announced as a little boy at the breakfast table that you were going to be a minister when you grew up! Today, Robert, my dream—and yours—has come true! We both know it was God's dream before it was ours!'

"That," I said to the proud cadets, "was the real secret of my success—and of yours. For all successful dreams start in the mind of God. And here's how they evolve. . . ."

Here Is How Dreams Evolve!

As I told the cadets, success is an evolution, not an overnight achievement; a journey, not a destination; an unending project, never a single, simple accomplishment that stands alone unrelated to the past and disconnected from the future. Success is a never-ending process of going through good times and bad, pleasure and pain, ups and downs, ins and outs!

I have observed that the successful achievement of a dream from conception to accomplishment evolves from Level One through Level Ten.

Level One: The Dream Actually Begins in the Mind of God.

Where do dreams begin? What is the ultimate source of inspiring ideas that somehow come into our minds to command our destinies?

I thought it was *my* dream to become a minister! Actually, as it turned out, it was my father's dream before it was my dream. He believed (and I share that faith) that it was God's dream before it was his or mine. And even as my dream came true at graduation when I became *The Reverend Robert Harold Schuller,* a new dream was born in my consciousness. It was a dream of finding a place in America where I could begin a church from scratch and devote my entire lifetime to that one job!

So when a call came—immediately after graduation— to help build a church in a Chicago suburb, I accepted. But after four years I received another invitation. This one was to begin a church—from scratch—in Orange County, California.

I never sought the invitation to begin the church. It came "out of the blue"—just as the quite uncommon compulsion to spend my entire life in one church had. So at the age of twenty-eight, with only my wife and five hundred dollars, I headed for California with an overpowering and overwhelming sense that I would begin a new, fantastic church!

But where did the dream come from? It came "out of the blue!" Dreams that capture our imaginations and inspire our wills begin in the mind of God.

Level Two: God Matches His Dream to the Dreamer.

God searches for the right person to whom he can entrust the greatest gift he can give a human being—a dream!

"I have an idea—a dream." He asks, "Who can I give it to? Who will receive it with respect, embrace it with a passion, and claim it as his own? Live for it? Die for it?"

The dreamer must be someone who will love the dream, even though it will make its dramatic entrance into that finite human mind as an awesome, impossible idea! The Almighty must find some person who will instinctively, intuitively, impulsively, passionately welcome the new dream into his heart, hugging the holy, happy possibility as something precious! A fresh love, a newborn child!

To whom can God entrust His dream? The wrong person would laugh it off or ridicule the impossible dream, rejecting it out of hand in sarcastic scorn. God must be careful where He drops the seed lest it fall on hard ground—a mind infected with cynicism. Or it might fall on shallow ground, where it could sprout but later die for lack of deep soil, in want of nourishment. God must avoid the mind that would welcome with instant enthusiasm the infant dream, only to abandon it in times of stress.

God must find the right mind to which He can send this impossible idea! Someone who will receive it; respect it; reverence it; research it; replenish it; reward it; reproduce it!

Yes—reproduce it—for no dream is ever *a* dream! Many apples will grow from one seed that is planted, nurtured, and nourished. So God finds a person whom He can make the steward of this, His new and exciting creative idea. The Almighty looks for a Possibility Thinker. Somewhere on planet Earth some simple, ordinary person working on the street, sitting behind a desk, jogging, bathing, reading, praying, crying, laughing suddenly gets a bright idea "out of the blue!" God has made His move. Contact has been made between heaven and earth. The divine creative process has asserted itself once more. Creation is eternal—like success, an unending process!

The same wonderful spirit that moved in the beginning of creation, bringing life onto a dead planet, brings life into otherwise dead spirits with the spark of a high and honorable vision of fabulous possibilities! At this point the dreamer picks up the dream and runs with it—he becomes a "Possibility Thinker"!

The divine dream is delegated to a dedicated doer!

Level Three: The Dream Takes on a Life of Its Own.

The dream now enters its gestation period. The dreamer becomes pregnant with what will become a new life. A beautiful new creation! A glorious achievement! A wonderful accomplishment! An awesome success!

God has given the dream a life of its own, like a fertilized seed which develops through many stages to become a human being about to be born. The success cycle is on its way!

Notice when success started. It had its beautiful beginning when the dreamer accepted the dream, when a human being welcomed the uninvited inspiring idea and embraced it as his own private possession! Do not move past that moment lightly, for that was a miracle moment! How easily that young boy of five could have dismissed the off-the-cuff comment from a heroic uncle just arriving from China!

Success begins once we start to believe in the beautiful dream that God sends us. How marvelous that our response was positive and not negative. How remarkable that the simple dream was not dismissed offhandedly as an impossibility, when in fact the moment was a meeting of a human mind with the dream of the Creator—God!

Once success starts it can never stop. For success is never ending. Even the setting of the sun does not mark an end to the day that is past, for that day is given eternal life as it becomes a part of irrevocable history!

How far will the dream travel? How long will its life span be? Will the new life that stirs in the womb go to full term and be born to live out a normal life span? Or will it be aborted intentionally or by accident or injury and labeled a miscarriage? Even so, it will be remembered. Positive ideas have instant immortality, even if they die in the womb. They have left their imprint in the memory. More often than not, the idea will be reborn, renewed! And if it amounts to nothing more than a temporary recollection, it will make a new impact on the human consciousness. So it isn't totally dead after all. It is really true—success is never ending and failure is never final!

So be sure of this: Once a dream has been embraced by the fertile, imaginative, dynamic mind of a Possibility Thinker, in that very moment something new has come into existence!

Level Four: God Times the Evolutionary Process.

The fourth dimension of a dream-in-process is timing.

Sometimes the gestation period is incredibly swift. More often it is geared to a schedule designed to teach the dreamer patience.

What is the single quality that more than any other identifies those who succeed? It is patience. Impatient dreamers will look for painless shortcuts and cheap discounts on the price of success! And failing to spot the expedient paths, unknowing, impatient dreamers will too often, too easily, and too painfully turn away from the divine dream. Later, when it's too late, they will discover that in choosing the painless, easy road they were in fact going down a primrose path to boredom, shame, emptiness, failure, poverty. If only they had not been afraid of the discipline that the dream demanded!

I will never know how valuable a gift God gave me when He presented my dream to me at such a young age that I would inevitably, unavoidably be forced to think in terms of decades! Nearly twenty years would pass before the mortarboard and tassel would be on my head and the glorious diploma placed trustfully and permanently into my waiting palm.

The deep groove of patience was indelibly carved into my mental attitude over those years of study and struggle. By the time I stepped from the halls of academia onto the sidewalk of the world where humanity struggles and strives, I was already accustomed to taking the long look. It would be easy for me to take a "forty-year look" toward my dream of establishing in my lifetime a truly great church for the glory of God.

Indeed, it took many years—almost a lifetime—for that dream to evolve and reach full bloom. The first five years of my ministry in Garden Grove, California, were a steady week-after-week effort to build a following by preaching from the rooftop of the snack bar of a drive-in theatre. The next ten years brought the acquisition of ten acres of land and the construction of our first church building, designed by the world-renowned architect, Richard Neutra. The following ten years saw the building of our church office complex in a facility named the Tower of Hope. This building, with its ninety-foot cross gleaming in the sky, became a landmark of hope at the freeway hub of Orange County in Southern California.

Success seemed to be never ending! For then came the dream of the Crystal Cathedral. Impossible! Incredible! So it seemed. But as I look back today I can only say that nothing is too great for the God who gives impossible dreams!

So, a church that started with two members, five hundred dollars, and the free use of a drive-in theatre, celebrated its twenty-fifth anniversary with the dedication of what has been called one of the truly great contemporary cathedrals on planet Earth. It was a media event. It was the crowning artistic achievement of Philip Johnson—one of the greatest architects of the twentieth century.

Level Five: Surprising Support Comes from Unexpected Sources.

The dream which has begun in the mind of God and is deposited in the mind of a Possibility Thinker suddenly begins to accrue support from sources, centers, and souls the dreamer never knew before. The dream, like a mighty majestic magnet, begins to attract help from persons who are motivated to help inspiring dreamers achieve success. The persons with the right strengths, skills, and spheres of influence come from out of the woodwork to move the dream forward, onward, and upward!

Like players on the stage these helpers make their dramatic entrances at the most propitious moments. Those who have worked closely with me through the years have heard me say a hundred or more times, "I am a success because God sends the right people with the right support at the right time."

At this stage of the dream God begins to build a team around it. People, power, and positive pressures will begin to move the idea from an impossibility to a possibility. We begin to witness the enormous mountain-moving energy that is generated when believing minds join to make a miracle happen.

Level Six: Temporary Setbacks and Difficulties Create Frustration.

By this point you were probably expecting final victory! Crowning achievement! Solid success! Hold on—you're not there—*yet!*

My testimony is that there must be a last-minute test and trial before the great triumphant moment of stunning success. I have always experienced pain, suffering, or costly difficulties at this stage. The dream and the dreamer experience setbacks, delays, and frustrations. This stage assures God that the dreamer will be truly humble when the crown is placed upon his head.

Carefully planned strategies may fail. All options may seem to have been used up. Has the dreamer failed? As of today—yes! But he can try again tomorrow. Failure is never final. Success does not need to end at this dismal moment of discouragement. It was in such a moment that I wrote, "When you think you have exhausted all possibilities, remember this: You haven't."

People and pressures shift. Obstacles will not be the same size tomorrow that they are today. Faced with a mountain? That's good! What's good about a mountain? It can't get any bigger! But you can! You may need to retreat, regroup, redesign, restructure, or reorganize for another assault on that steep, slippery peak! And you will! You may need to return to the God who gave you the dream in the first place. Find your faith renewed in His promises:

- "I can do all things through Christ who strengthens me" (Phil. 4:13).
- "If God is for us, who can be against us?" (Rom. 8:31).

You have hope! A new day will bring breakthroughs. Your aspirations will be affirmed by new powers and people that God will send your way. He has not brought you so far only to abandon you. He is simply preparing you for Level Seven.

Level Seven: The Dream Comes True!

Stunning success is bestowed upon your praying, your possibility thinking, your patience, and your pain! You have arrived. The business is established. The career is firmly grounded. Now be prepared for surprises—and disappointments! Honors as well as hurts will come unsought and uninvited. Enthusiastic applause will come from your supporters. However, when you have reached the top of the mountain, you will also be noticed by your competitors. Jealousy will swing against you. Opponents and envious peers will lash out at you.

You will be prepared because you have already been scarred in the climb upward. You are a veteran. You are a seasoned mountain climber. Your problem will not be arrogance or destructive pride but maintaining the self-confidence that what you've done has been right, honorable, noble, and good!

I have often had to tell the youthful dreamer that possibility thinking does not lead to haughty pride. By the time the dreamer has succeeded, the quality of humility will be so deeply entrenched in his personality that his modesty will be honest. When your positive pride is rooted in the grace and goodness of God, your humility is guaranteed! Yes: The process of success has carried you to the top! This must be the last level in the evolution of the dream. Right? Wrong.

Level Eight: The Dreamer Has Been Shaped by the Dream.

The dreamer has arrived now at the upper stratum. He looks in the mirror—and is shocked! He discovers that he has been changed, shaped, carved, and molded by the dream! He has become as great as—and no greater than—the dream that has driven him, consumed him, and become incarnate in his very personality. Now he understands that there are no great people—only ordinary people. Some simply have bigger dreams than others. Now we see how dreamers are really rewarded.

The pain they encountered along the way has given them more compassion for the hurts of others. The unexpected support from unforeseen sources has caused them to grow in their faith in both God and their fellow human beings. The tenacity that sustained them through the tough and terrible times has left them with far greater patience and tolerance. Their deepest motive—to help people who are hurting—has etched gentleness and tenderness on their well-traveled faces. Living the dream has changed them! They are richer, fuller, broader people because they dreamed the dream and stayed with it.

So when you choose the dream, the dream will decide

your destiny. The size of the dream will determine how big a person you will become.

Level Nine: The Dream Keeps Growing!

In this phase the curtain opens to give a vision of tomorrow. The dreamer learns that great dreams of great dreamers are never fulfilled—they are transcended! Hence, they tend to propagate themselves. Success multiplies. It is never ending!

Having made the dream come true, you discover that success is not an end in itself, but a positioning in power for greater accomplishments and loftier achievements. For example, financial security only provides a broader base for larger efforts that would never have been possible or imagined before.

Your academic degree is in your hand? The dream has come true? For what end? Simply to frame an important document in your private office? Of course not. Rather it is to give you the base to move forward, upward, and onward. Now you can be taken seriously by serious people.

This is the time to stop and reappraise your power. Review your assets. Subtract your liabilities from your assets and find out what your net worth is today—in professional terms, in intellectual terms, in experience and knowledge, in financial terms.

You may be astounded by your strength. You have a power base for leverage against mountains that you never would have tackled before. You are in a tremendously powerful position to dream greater dreams. In addition, the people whom you have helped along the way will not let you quit. So be prepared for the tenth and final level of dreaming.

Level Ten: The Dreamer Enters the Danger Zone.

This is the perilous time. The dreamer is now in danger of not keeping up with a fast-growing, forward-looking dream. The dream—like a growing child—is in danger of running ahead of him—as the scholar outruns the master, as the athlete outruns the trainer. The dream now is taking

command. And meanwhile the dreamer wants to rest, re-
tire—at least take a sabbatical.

"Come on!" The racing, growing dream calls out to the
weary dreamer. "There are more heights to climb. Can't you
see them? There are more victories to be won."

The dreamer hesitates. He wants to rest, but he must
not. At this point he needs a new dream. Once again, he must
go through the ten phases. He knows that if he doesn't continue to dream and grow, then he will begin to die. As the
poet Evangeline Wilkes has poignantly put it:

> On the sands of hesitation,
> Lay the bones of countless millions,
> Who at the dawn of victory
> Sat down to wait,
> And waiting—died!

When you reach Level Ten—BEWARE! TAKE CARE!
And accept a new DARE! I dare you to start dreaming again!
When the alternative to dreaming is dying, then the decision
should be easy!

So where do you get a new dream? Go back to Level
One. Go to the quiet corner where you will encounter the
God who put you here in the first place. Report back to the
Source of all great, grand, and good dreams!

I speak from personal experience, for I recently emerged
from this danger zone. When the Cathedral was dedicated,
the people, the parishioners, and the press all asked me,
"What's your next dream?"

I really didn't have an answer. The truth is I had no
further plans. The emotional toll had left me limp and empty.
Embracing the dream of an all-glass cathedral, with its fabulous possibilities, and never once contemplating compromise, but striving for excellence in art and architecture had
drained me. I hardly had enough energy to show any enthusiasm that September morning in 1980 when the Cathedral
was dedicated to the glory of man for the greater glory of
God!

Privately, I poured my heart out to my one intimate,
essential friend, my wife. "Everybody wants Schuller to have

a bigger dream. But I'm tired, Arvella. I'm exhausted. My motives for building the Cathedral have been criticized. Cynical people and sincere friends have attacked the amount of money spent. I don't have it in me anymore to dream. Besides, haven't I done enough with my one life?"

For the first time in my life I felt that my dreams had come true—completely. I had succeeded. I knew it. It was enough. Put a period behind that word "success." That's how I punctuated my progress. But I was wrong. It's not the nature of success to stop! I would have to learn a big lesson—success is never ending! I mistakenly assumed that the days of dreaming dreams were past for me. But when I was celebrating my sixtieth birthday my only son, Robert Anthony Schuller, said to me, "Dad, you haven't finished building your church. You have an office facility—the beautiful Tower of Hope. You have a wonderful church in the Crystal Cathedral. But you have never built a center with Christian education facilities that can minister to family needs and insure the future generations of the church."

"But I don't have the land," I protested.

"Purchase the apartment complex that's next to the Cathedral."

"But that's *impossible*, Bob," I heard myself say. Our eyes locked together instantly in shock at hearing that word so foreign to my vocabulary.

"Impossible!" We both laughed. "Try again," my son urged. He knew that I had previously failed in attempts to purchase the apartment units that occupied four acres of adjacent land. The owner would not sell. I had failed. Besides, who needed any more success?

But success will never stop. It continues to produce new possibilities—sometimes in the form of new problems. Failure must never be final! Try again!

Alone with my thoughts and my prayers, I telephoned a real estate agent and urged him to make an all-out effort to purchase the complex. "We're willing to pay six million dollars," I confided.

This time the owner was of a different mood and mind. New tax laws going into effect at the end of the year would make it advantageous for him to sell. We agreed on a price of $5 million. After one call to the bank we had instant and total financing.

Once again I was dreaming! I began to imagine a building on our newly enlarged piece of real estate that could serve the needs of the church as well as future generations. But then a new question arose: How could we connect this new structure to the Crystal Cathedral to present a total composition that would be united in spirit, style, and structure?

A vague image began to take shape in my mind. It was the image of yet another structure. I called Philip Johnson. "Philip, the dream's not over as I had thought. You've got to complete the Crystal Cathedral." My voice was passionate. "We have the church, we have the people, but where's the steeple?"

Although I laughed as I said it, I was serious as I continued. "Mr. Johnson, we need a steeple, expertly designed and rightly positioned next to the Cathedral to tie the whole property together. In the prayer chapel that will be located at its base we can launch a new ministry of twenty-four-hour prayer. In addition it will serve to unite the Crystal Cathedral with the new Family Center we will be constructing on the land we have recently acquired."

Philip picked up the idea and designed what may be the most stunning and spectacular church spire ever to be dreamed by an architect. The plans have been drawn up. City approval has been granted, and for the next few years I will be raising the funds necessary to develop the plan and make the dream come true. Past failures to enlarge our real estate have been overcome by the greater power of Possibility Thinking! So, today I can write with integrity: *"Success is never ending; failure is never final."*

Will dreaming ever end? Not if we allow God to have His way and to set His own timetable! Even as I write this book, I am standing on tiptoes, looking over the edge of tomorrow to see the happy fulfillment of my life's dream!

Where is your life today? On which level are you? Wherever you are, I offer you these encouraging words: *Daring to dream means daring to live!* You can be a dreamer and a doer too! You can watch your dreams come true, and from personal experience I can tell you it's very exciting!

- Once I had a dream that I would build a great church! The Crystal Cathedral is standing today.
- Once I had a dream of building a national television ministry. Today the Hour of Power, the number one rated television ministry in America, reaches millions each week.
- Once I had a dream that I would become a successful author. I have had the tremendous satisfaction of seeing four of my books make the *New York Times, Time* magazine, and *Publishers Weekly* best-selling lists.
- Once I had a dream that I would have a happy marriage and healthy and successful children. Today my wife and I have been married for thirty-seven years. We love each other more than yesterday—but less than tomorrow. My five children? All of them are successful! All of them are dreamers. All of them are doers. All of them are Possibility Thinkers.
- Today I have a NEW dream—a dream of completing the Crystal Cathedral by building a 234-foot glass spire that will sparkle and shimmer in the sun and sparkle like stars in the night. It is going to happen! For I have been able to DREAM it—and therefore we will be able to DO it!

Yes, my greatest dream is still on the drawing board! Success is never ending! And it starts when you dare to dream a beautiful dream. So join me. If you can dream it, you can do it too!

*May You Live
As Long As
You Want*

*And Want
As Long As
You Live!*

CHAPTER 3

If You Can DREAM It

You Can DO It!

No matter *where* you are in life—
No matter *who* you are—
No matter *what* you have accomplished—
No matter *when* or *where* or *why* you may have failed—
I challenge you to answer the following questions:
- What dreams would you be setting for yourself if you knew you could not fail?
- What goals would you have on the drawing board if you had unlimited financial resources?
- What plans would you be making if you knew you could "pull them off"?
- What projects would you be launching if you had the wisdom to solve any problem and the power to sweep all obstacles out of your way?
- What exciting work would you be engaged in today if you could acquire the skill to sell your ideas to powerful people?

ANYBODY can dream! ANYBODY can plan! As it says

in the song, "When you wish upon a star, makes NO DIF-
FERENCE WHO YOU ARE!"

Success will be never ending and failure will never be
final for those people who have the capacity to dream.

In 1955 when I arrived in California to begin a church,
only two miles away Walt Disney was burning orange trees
to build a place called Disneyland. On my wall I have this
line from my celebrated neighbor: "Somehow I can't believe
there are many heights that can't be scaled by a man who
knows the secret of making dreams come true. This special
secret can be summarized in four C's. They are: *curiosity,
confidence, courage,* and *constancy,* and the greatest of these
is confidence."

Walt Disney knew the secret of making his dreams come
true. It's possible for you to make yours come true too!

Everything starts, of course, with an idea or a dream.
Everybody has ideas pass through their minds. The only difference is what they do with those ideas.

The truth is that many of you have seen someone do
something great and thought, "How did they do that?"

Perhaps you had the idea, too, but you did nothing
about it. The great people are no different from you or me;
they simply grabbed a great idea before it disappeared into
oblivion. They took an option out on it. They wrote it down
so they wouldn't forget it. It became a dream. Then, intuitively or through training, they learned how to make their
dreams come true. They had the four C's!

You Can Dream—If You Have CURIOSITY!

What single quality do we find in the mental activity of
all dreamers and doers? "Creative curiosity." Curiosity is the
dynamic portion of the mind that provokes the questions
that release creativity.

For millenia people sat under trees, only to have apples
fall and hit them on the head. For millenia the human response was predictable:

"Ouch!"

Or, "Gosh! What an apple!"

Then one day, according to the legend, a man was hit on the head by an apple, and he responded with creative curiosity. He asked, "Why? Why did the apple fall down instead of rising up and floating away like a cloud, a feather, or a leaf? Why do leaves fly away while apples fall down?"

That curiosity led Newton to discover the law of gravity!

In the twenty years since I wrote my "textbook," *Move Ahead with Possibility Thinking,* I have received responses from thousands of persons who tried Possibility Thinking and found that it released the capacity to be creative! Curiosity turned them into problem solvers and decision makers.

The Right Questions Release Possibilities

Just think what happens if you ask possibility reviewing questions like:
- Why is it impossible?
- What would it take to turn this impossibility into a possibility?
- Where could financing be found to make it possible?
- Would it be possible if I had the right team? Materials? Deadline extension?

The Right Questions Release Confidence

Start asking questions that reflect creative curiosity— curiosity questions to build your self-confidence or rebuild your faltering or fractured self-respect:
- If others can go from nothing to something, why can't I?
- If others have moved out of their poverty into prosperity, why can't I?
- If others who had academic records as bad as or worse than mine went back to earn educations and become lawyers, ministers, accountants, and doctors, why can't I?
- If others have been forgiven, restored, and rehabilitated, why can't I make a comeback too?
- If I try it again, start over once more, won't I be a wiser person the next time around? Can't I learn from

my mistakes and failures? Can't I turn them into positive forces for personal improvement? If so, my failure won't be final at all—only a pause for reorganization!

The Right Questions Release Creative Solutions

Ask questions that lead you to people who are smarter than you are:
- Who in the world could possibly figure out a solution to this problem?
- What kind of skills and talents do I need to turn this problem into a possibility?

Ask questions that might clarify distortions in your thinking.
- Is the problem as serious as I am making it?
- What's the worst that could happen? Can I live with that? And if I think not, why not? Others are! Why couldn't I?
- If worse comes to worst, can I still turn this obstacle into an opportunity? The scar into a star?

The Right Questions Release Motivation

Ask questions that can turn you into a self-starter. Remember, nobody else can motivate you until you motivate yourself. Ask questions that generate energy deep from within your being, such as:
- If I simply made a start—could I accomplish just a little bit?
- If I accomplish a little bit, will that be the beginning of something that can slowly or swiftly be expanded? If I save dollars, will they not accumulate and be multiplied? How long will it take before a little bit of money invested, compounded with interest, will give me a down payment to get started?
- If I start my days earlier, work later, put in more time and effort, what will happen?

I was a student in theological seminary when I was introduced to a minister who started as a young man in a

church with only about thirty members. But he spent over
forty years in that one church. When he completed his ministry, it was the largest Baptist church in the world—the
First Baptist Church in Dallas, Texas. His name was George
Truett.

That story provoked my curiosity: *What would happen
if I spent my whole life in one church? And if I kept building
year after year, decade after decade, achievement upon
achievement, where could that lead?*

Out of those questions the dream to build a great church
was born! When I came to California without money or
members and could find no empty building to rent, I noticed
the drive-through windows at banks, as well as the drive-in
theatres. The *curious* question that came into my mind was,
"Would a drive-in church work? If not, why not? And if anybody could do it, why not I?"

Out of the creative questions came the dream of a drive-
in church. Out of the motivating questions came the energy
to see the dream through. Out of the possibility questions
came the solutions until the dream came true.

Curiosity is a necessity for every dreamer and every
doer!

You Can Dream—If You Have Confidence!

In addition to curiosity, the dreamer needs confidence.
So tap into the power of five magic words: "I CAN DO IT
TOO!"

Verbalize these enthusiasm-producing words. Say them
aloud—to yourself! Announce them to your positive-thinking friends: "I CAN DO IT TOO!"

Have confidence in yourself as well as in your dream.
Dreamers who become doers operate emotionally and ra-
tionally with (a) confidence in their *intelligence*, (b) confidence in their hidden *instincts*, and (c) confidence in their
silent and secret *intuition*.

Intelligence, instinct, and intuition all can be instruments of divine guidance, and we can have confidence if we
believe that our wonderful, positive ideas are created in the

mind of God. "Be confident of this very thing, that He who has begun a good work in you will complete it" (Phil. 1:6).

Have confidence in whatever *intelligence* you have. But do not confuse *education* with *intelligence*. Real intelligence is rooted in the subconscious and is the ability to recognize and respond enthusiastically to positive possibilities. Such intelligence is an inherited or acquired sensitivity to perceive universal principles and to respond creatively by applying those principles forthrightly.

Education is the acquisition of knowledge. As important as it is, knowledge cannot take the place of wisdom, for wisdom is the ability to use knowledge intelligently. Recognize that *formal education* may or may not be a solid basis for responsible self-confidence. If the academic degrees have increased knowledge but have diminished wisdom, then formal education has become counterproductive. Not a few persons with advanced degrees have acquired facts and knowledge but have been mentally conditioned to negative thinking by cynical and negative-thinking professors.

Unfortunately and unnecessarily too many educated persons with impressive diplomas are at the bottom of every ladder. Above them can be found a surprising number of persons with less formal education. The difference is an added awareness that attitude is more important than knowledge.

Although facts are the lifeblood of knowledge, attitude is the lifeblood of wisdom. Indeed, the beginning and the end, the alpha and the omega, of accomplishment is wisdom.

So Possibility Thinking is the positive mental conditioning of human attitudes to produce wisdom. And when we have the wisdom to be a Possibility Thinker, we are wise indeed. Now, let us add to wisdom all of the knowledge we can acquire, but knowledge without the wisdom of a positive mental attitude will produce an educated negative thinker, which explains why a formal education is not enough.

It comes down to this. If you will make a deliberate decision to develop a positive attitude toward opportunities and obstacles, you are on your way toward having what is the most important quality in education: the power of positive thinking.

Now that you have confidence in your self-confidence, you can have confidence in what you've learned in life. That's education, whether acquired in the classroom or in the "school of hard knocks" or by authentic experience. Keep on getting as smart as you can—and smarter! Either acquire knowledge to manage your dreams successfully or know where to go to find people who are smarter than you are—people who can provide legal counsel, financial counsel, or other technical knowledge. Success goes to people who are super-smart Possibility Thinkers!

Now have confidence in your *instincts*. Someone said, "When God wants to guarantee a truth in one of his creatures, he ingrains the reality in their instinct." A bird creates its nest. A salmon returns to its place of origin. A human being operates successfully on "hunches" best described as instinctive.

Is such instinctive behavior a part of what is often called intuition? Perhaps it is. If so, then have confidence in your intuition. It has been my privilege to learn from and become friends with some of the greatest psychiatrists of our century. I once asked Dr. Victor Frankl, who was then head of psychiatry at the University of Vienna, Austria, "What is intuition?" His answer was simple and honest: "Nobody knows." I asked the same question of Dr. Karl Menninger. Same answer.

The psychiatrist Scott Peck pointed out in his book *The Road Less Traveled,* "The subconscious is always ahead of the conscious." Is intuition an emotional judgment that has been made by the subconscious which accumulates all of our experiences, observations, perceptions, including the entire memory bank of living and learning?

I suggest that any explanation of intuition or instinct which fails to acknowledge the presence and power of God is indeed shortsighted and intellectually irresponsible. My simple testimony is that I have prayed for simple guidance all my life in everything that I have thought and done. Consequently, I have learned to trust my God-given instincts.

We hired Philip Johnson to design the Crystal Cathedral because he is, in my opinion, the greatest architect in the world. In our first meeting I told him that I wanted an all-glass church so people could see in and out. Elaborating, I said, "I think a healthy person who is emotionally and spiritually mature will be an open person. Let the structure make that statement."

Soon I received a call from Philip. He was eager to show me his first plans. They called for an all-glass roof supported by solid walls. Frankly, I was less than enthusiastic. Philip sensed my lack of excitement and said, "What's wrong?"

I covered my true feelings. I said, "Nothing."

He protested, "C'mon, Bob. Why aren't you more excited?"

I was afraid to be honest with him. I said as much to Philip: "Sir, who am I, a minister, to challenge the world's greatest architect?"

He looked sternly at me and said, "Bob, if we want to work together, you better learn one thing right now, and don't you ever forget it." He stared long and hard at me.

"What is it?" I asked.

"Architecture is too important to leave up to the architect."

That gave me the confidence to speak up. "Well, I wanted the walls to be glass, too."

The result? Philip went back to the drawing board and created one of his greatest masterpieces—the Crystal Cathedral.

Architecture is too important to leave to the architects. Education is too important to leave to the educators. Science is too important to leave to the scientists. The whole subject of war and peace is too important to leave to the state department and the military experts. Business is too important to leave to the businesspersons. The economy (especially when you pay the bills) is too important to leave to the economists. Surely, religion is too important to leave to the theologians. Creativity is too important to leave to artists.

So—dare to believe that your ideas are worthwhile. And

have confidence in your God-given instincts. More often than not they will be right!

You Can Dream—If You Have COURAGE!

Jeb Stuart was a loyal follower of General Robert E. Lee. He was a courageous officer and a man of integrity who always signed his letters to the general, "You can count on me, Jeb."

Frankly, that's the commitment I've made to my God who gives me positive ideas. I have prayed, "If You will entrust the dream to me, Lord, *You can count on me!* I won't let it fly away. I'll do something with it. I will give it the best that I can!"

Courage? Yes. Integrity? Absolutely! I spell courage, I-N-T-E-G-R-I-T-Y, for courage is really *honesty.* When you see someone who's operating with real courage, they are actually exhibiting integrity. They have to do what they're doing or they would be disloyal. I hope you will come to believe, as I do, that our dreams are *entrusted* to our care and keeping by God—with the obligation to turn ideas into creative action. Then, as an honest trustee, you will be so motivated by integrity that you'll have no place for fear.

I learned this lesson as a child growing up on a farm where we raised milk cows. They had to be milked every morning and every night without a single exception! "Come hell or high water," as the farmers put it. No matter what! And it was my chore to milk. No problem ever got in the way of doing what I had to do.

Call that responsibility. Call it accountability. It adds up to integrity. And integrity leaves little room for fear. And when that negative emotion threatens, turn it into a positive force. Here's how:

Fear not that you might fail . . . *Fear rather* that you might never succeed if you never dare to try.

Fear not that you might make a mistake believing in your dream . . . *Fear rather* that if you don't go for it you might stand before God and He'll tell you that you could have succeeded if you'd had more faith.

Fear not that if it doesn't work out you'll be embarrassed . . . *Fear rather* that if you don't try that time will only prove you could have succeeded! The saddest words of tongue or pen are these: "It might have been."

Fear not that you might fail . . . *Fear rather* that you will never succeed if you don't start taking risks.

Fear not that you might be hurt . . . *Fear rather* that you might never grow if you keep waiting for painless success.

Fear not that you might love and lose . . . *Fear rather* that you might never love at all.

Fear not that others might laugh at your mistakes . . . *Fear rather* that God will say to you, "O you of little faith."

Fear not that you might fall again . . . *Fear rather* that you might have made it the next time if you'd only tried once more and given it all you had.

Failure doesn't mean you were dumb to try; it means you had courage to explore and experiment to see what would work and what would not. Failure doesn't mean you don't know how to make decisions; it just means you have to make another decision. You can overcome the fear of failure when you re-define that word:

Failure doesn't mean you are a failure . . . It does mean you haven't succeeded yet.

Failure doesn't mean you have accomplished nothing . . . It does mean you have learned something.

Failure doesn't mean you have been a fool . . . It does mean you had a lot of faith.

Failure doesn't mean you've been disgraced . . . It does mean you were willing to try.

Failure doesn't mean you don't have it . . . It does mean you have to do something in a different way.

Failure doesn't mean you are inferior . . . It does mean you are not perfect.

Failure doesn't mean you've wasted your life . . . It does mean you have a reason to start afresh.

Failure doesn't mean you should give up . . . It does mean you must try harder.

Failure doesn't mean you'll never make it . . . It does mean it will take a little longer.

Failure doesn't mean God has abandoned you . . . It does mean God has a better idea![1]

Failure doesn't mean you're finished . . . It does mean you have a chance to try something new.

So it's true! Failure is never final!

Do you want to stay where you are the rest of your life? God has bigger and better things for you and me, but we'll never advance until we take a chance. Taking a chance means running the risk of personal failure and real hurt. It requires courage.

I ran into a young man in an airport in Texas. He happened to be carrying a copy of my book, *Tough Times Never Last But Tough People Do.* He recognized me, came up to me, and said: "Can I have your autograph?"

Of course I was glad to give it to him.

"Dr. Schuller," he said, "this book has really helped me. I'm in absolute bankruptcy. I started my own business, but I've lost everything I ever had." He had a tear in his eye, but he continued. "My business was going pretty good. I expanded with a new plant and more equipment. I was making quite a bit. Suddenly the other people who owed me money didn't pay. The little businesses went down the tubes. Then a couple of big businesses went under. I looked at my accounts receivable, and suddenly everything I had expected to take in had withered away. My accounts receivable were worth nothing. When that happened, I went under too. That's where I am today. But your book is helping."

I looked at this intelligent young businessman and said, "First of all, let me correct you. You haven't lost everything you had."

"Oh," he said, "but I have!"

"No," I protested, "I don't think so. You had something before you had a business. You had a dream. And you had the nerve to try. You haven't lost that."

He said, "I think I have."

I argued, "Oh, no! Nobody ever loses courage! Courage

---

[1]Robert Schuller, *You Can Become the Person You Want to Be* (New York: Hawthorn Books, Inc., 1973), 73.

is something you can never lose, because courage is something you can always choose!"

The truth is that courage isn't a gift. Courage is a DECISION! Courage is not the absence of fear, it is the presence of a calling—a dream that pulls you beyond yourself. Hence it is something you can never lose. It is always something that you can choose. So, choose it today!

You Can Dream—If You Can Maintain CONSTANCY!

Follow it through, wrap it up, complete the work, never pack up. I came to California thirty years ago with a forty-year plan. That's what I call *onstancy*. Stick with your dream even if you get knocked down. Tap into the incredible power generated by an uncompromising commitment to constancy!

In the first thirty years of my ministry I could pinpoint more than a dozen times when, for a variety of reasons, I wanted to walk away! I would have given anything if I could have quit! Run away! Never come back! What kept me from leaving my dream, turning my back on it? A Bible verse, for one thing: "No one, having put his hand to the plow, and looking back, is fit for the kingdom of God" (Luke 9:62). And another thought: "When things get rough, don't move. People and pressures shift, but the soil remains the same no matter where you go."

Finally, I was and am a great believer in "base building." Walk away and you lose whatever base you have built—goodwill, professional connections, community respect, firsthand knowledge of an area or activity—an accumulated power that would be tough to discard. Troubles pass, but bases are tough to replace. Constancy means "stick-to-it-iveness" and "follow-through." Every salesperson knows this is what separates winners from losers. "Follow-through"—every successful manager knows that without constant review and rechecking great projects can fall into little cracks and die before they're rescued.

I was ministering to the military in the Orient during the

Vietnam War. The headquarters of the medical evacuation effort were located in Tachekawa, Japan. The commanding general shared with me how successful their efforts had been in the Vietnamese War. "I will tell you something you'll find hard to believe, Dr. Schuller," the commanding general said. "But in this war we have only lost eleven lives in transit. We studied the fatalities in the Korean War and World War II and noticed that many deaths occurred while a patient was being moved: in planes, trains, ambulances, boats. Understandably, we are limited in what we can do to save a life if we're in the air or on the road. So we never let the helicopter take off or allowed the ambulance to roll until we were sure the patient could withstand the trip. Now, Dr. Schuller, step into our command room and you'll see three words that have saved thousands of lives, three words that every doctor, nurse, and litter bearer has to live by."

I stepped into a huge room, half the size of a football field. On one wall was a map of the Orient, the Pacific, and America. Lights blinked where hospital and transportation lines were in place. And above the entire wall, from one end to another, were three words with letters that must have been six to eight feet high. The three lifesaving words were, "CHECK—DOUBLE-CHECK—RECHECK."

"Often we caught the problem in our third checking and saved a life!" the general explained. That's follow-through!

Another word that illustrates constancy is "bounce-back-ability." Your enthusiasm may dip for a moment, your excitement level may rise and fall, but you will never become so depressed and discouraged that you quit.

I know your dream may have been smashed. The company has gone bankrupt, or you've been passed by for promotion. Perhaps the marriage is over, or you lost the love of your life. Your dream has died. Now what do you do?

Believe in the power of God to give you a new dream, to help you make a mark for good while you still live. And bear in mind that *if you can dream it—you can do it!* Time and again I have seen this principle at work! YOU CAN DO IT!

Henry Ford said, "Think you can, think you can't; either way you'll be right."

"I can!" said the retired postman.

He was a rural mailman for twenty years. But when he retired after two decades of postal service in Makanda, Illinois, Wayman Presley had acquired a small pension and $1,100 in savings. Today, at 82, he is a millionaire. His travel company does nearly $7 million in sales a year with Presley Tours all across the nation.

How does a retired mailman become a prosperous businessman? He did it by believing in himself and his abilities and by making others happy. He always loved to take friends and neighbors on hiking trips and teach them about the flowers and trees. The trips gradually became more and more organized, including meals and snacks.

One day someone said to him, "I would love to see the ocean." That simple wish enthusiastically expressed to Wayman Presley led to a tour of 546 people to Miami Beach. Wayman made $120 and had such a good time that he decided to go into a travel business that has become one of the largest in the country. He has made a name for himself. He has made a lot of money for his family. He has created jobs for hundreds and showed God's beautiful world to thousands!

"I can!" said the young wife and mother.

Marie Callender was making potato salad and cole slaw in a delicatessen in Los Angeles during World War II. Her boss asked her to make pies for the lunch crowd. That was the start of a new career for Marie.

At first she baked the pies at home, dragging flour sacks that weighed over a hundred pounds each. Then in 1948 she and her husband sold their car and bought a Quonset hut, an oven, and a refrigerator. There she baked pies that her husband delivered to restaurants in the area. She started out baking about ten pies a day. Two years later, she was baking over two hundred pies a day. Sixteen years later, several thousand were coming out of the oven each day.

Marie and her husband opened their first pie shop in Orange County in 1964. That first year they barely broke even, but her husband and later her son helped guide the business until the chain of restaurants spread through fourteen states. In no time people were talking about Marie Callender's pies. They were undoubtedly the best to be found anywhere! And other items added to the menu were also exceptional in quality and taste.

In 1986 Ramada Inns, Inc., bought the family business—115 restaurants—from Marie and her son for $90 million. It was a tremendous accomplishment! Who would have thought that a young mother, armed with a rolling pin and a sack of flour, could have brought such delicious delight to so many people, not to mention thousands of jobs for bakers, cooks, waiters, and waitresses?

YOU CAN do it, too! YOU CAN make your dreams come true! YOU CAN build a new life! YOU CAN start over—even if you are down and out!

Yes, you can be a dreamer and a doer too, if you will remove one word from your vocabulary: *Impossible.*

*Courage Is
Something
You
Can Never Lose*

*Because
Courage Is
Something
You
Can Always Choose!*

CHAPTER 4

Nothing Is Impossible!

Nothing is impossible!

"Come on, Dr. Schuller!" you may say. "You're an educated man. How can you say that 'nothing is impossible'? Have you set aside the critical part of your brain?"

It's been widely reported that I have cut that word "impossible" out of my dictionary. That's true. I have, for more than one reason. To begin with it is *more often than not* used flippantly, frivolously, foolishly, and fruitlessly. No, I have not set aside the critical faculties of my brain. It is precisely because I have sharpened and honed these critical faculties that I have declared the word *impossible* out of bounds!

The fact that we don't know how something can be done does not mean we are smart or right to say, "It's impossible!" The fact that "experts" in the field say, "It's impossible," doesn't mean they're right.

I must warn you against the most dangerous and destructive force on earth—the Negative Thinking Expert.

Because he is an expert you will be tempted to listen uncritically, trust him, and quit! Struck by the authoritative position he holds, you will tend to believe him without question. Too often we hear through our peers, not through our ears!

Herbert Bayer, the 78-year-old artist, architect, designer, and author, gives us a poignant look at what would happen to art if a Negative Thinking Expert were to have his way. Here is Herbert's favorite figment, as described by John Dreyfuss, *Los Angeles Times* architecture and design critic:

> *An efficiency expert once took a step toward his ulcer by attending a performance of Schubert's "Unfinished" Symphony.*
>
> *"All 12 violins were playing identical notes," he complained. "This seems to be unnecessary duplication. The staff of this section should be drastically cut."*
>
> *Furthermore, the expert peevishly noted, the wind section's four oboes often were silent. His solution: Fire some of the oboists and "spread their work over the whole orchestra."*
>
> *With ingenuity surpassing reason, the efficiency man then observed that playing numerous 32nd notes seems "an excessive refinement," and they should be "rounded up to the nearest 16th note" so Schubert's work could be handled by "trainees in lower-grade orchestras."*
>
> *Warming to his subject, he decided that "no useful purpose is served by repeating with horns the passages that have already been handled with strings. If all such redundant passages were eliminated, the concert could be reduced from two hours to 20 minutes."*
>
> *Finally, the fellow wrapped his recommendations in a grand justification: "If Schubert had attended to these matters, he would probably have been able to finish the symphony."*[1]

---

[1] *Los Angeles Times,* © 1979. Reprinted by permission.

A Negative Thinking Expert is someone who is so well informed, trained, and experienced on the subject that if it's never been successfully done before, he'll know it and will not hesitate a moment to tell you. He will then, with the authoritative hauteur of a brilliant intellectual snob, enumerate all of the real or imaginary reasons why an idea never succeeded, convincing first himself, then you, that all of his words are proof positive that the whole notion is unrealistic, beyond credibility, ridiculous, unthinkable, and impossible. Thus he blocks progress, obstructs development, stifles creativity, halts advance thinking, and delays for months, years, or decades the big breakthroughs.

A Possibility Thinking Expert is a person who, when faced with a new concept and knowing that it has never been successfully implemented, is charged with excitement at what he sees as a great opportunity to become a pace-setting pioneer. He is stimulated by the opportunity to discover new solutions to old problems using the knowledge of a new age to make a historic breakthrough. Because he is convinced that there must be a way to overcome seemingly insurmountable difficulties, his creative powers are stimulated to produce amazing results. Using advanced research techniques, he proves that some long-accepted causes for past failure were, in fact, errors of judgment made by intelligent researchers who lacked the tools, skills, or related knowledge available in this modern age.[2] So failure is never final!

Just because some Negative Thinking Expert says, "I can't imagine it!" that doesn't mean that someone, somewhere, sometime cannot and will not be able to "imagine the unimaginable" and, amazingly, accomplish it!

I charge that too often progress has been halted, obstructed, and delayed by persons who used that word "impossible."

- "Transplant a human heart?! Impossible!"
- "Put a man on the moon?! Come on now. Impossible!"

---

[2]Schuller, *You Can Become*, 30, 31.

- "Build an all-glass cathedral longer than a football field, and make it earthquake proof in California?! That's impossible!"

No. I haven't placed the intellectual, rational half of my brain in reverse or neutral. I simply have lived my life in the twentieth century and have seen scientific impossibilities die like caterpillars, only to be born again as Possibility Butterflies.

You may tell me, "As of today there is no known way this could be accomplished." I'll buy that! That's an intelligent statement. But don't say, "It's impossible."

You may tell me that some new idea is completely unbelievable, absurd, ludicrous. Like doubting Thomas you won't believe until you have put your finger in the wound in Christ's hand! Okay! Okay! I can understand how you could react that way. But please don't paint yourself into a corner where you may have to "eat crow" someday. Whatever you do, don't use that word "impossible."

Be honest with me. Tell me if you just don't like the idea. It's not your style? Level with me and with yourself. Is your ego clouding your judgment? Maybe there's a "cross-cultural conflict" going on. Get to the real reasons. But don't use that unintelligent word "impossible"!

You may prove to me that the idea would not be cost effective. It would definitely not be profitable. But please tell me how, when, or by whom it might possibly become a "break-even" venture. And don't try to second-guess me. Maybe we'll want to do it even if it costs us money. So don't use that word "impossible"!

You may bring me this report: "It's been tried, and it has failed." I'll want to know (a) when, (b) where, (c) by whom, (d) and how. Then I'll want to review their work. But don't insult my intelligence by saying, "It's impossible!"

You may tell me that the laws as they stand *today* do not allow this. That's all right! That's smart! I appreciate this. But laws can be changed, so don't tell me, "It's impossible."

If in your mind the idea is immoral or unethical, then that's a different story altogether. Then we can agree. Let's use the word "unacceptable." But we won't use what would still be an incorrect word: "impossible."

I was on my third visit to Peking, China. On earlier trips I had fallen in love with one of the greatest art treasures in all of China, the famous bronze horse of the Han dynasty. It has been reproduced in small six-inch and twelve-inch sizes by the thousands. I had my heart set on having one that was four feet long. It would stand in our church retreat center in Hawaii. It would, more than any other art piece I could imagine, symbolize "The Free Spirit!" All my efforts to find and purchase such a large piece ran into negative stone walls as solid and immovable as the Great Wall! Finally I went to the top—the National Arts and Crafts Department that controlled the original. I was immediately given a one-word answer. You guessed it! They have learned that word in China, too, which is shocking when you see the *impossible* things they have done—in history, art, architecture, engineering! Well, out came the word, "Dr. Schuller, what you ask is *impossible.*"

Now let me explain what was going on in this "authority's" mind.

A. The request was unusual and would require special committee approval. This could be difficult. And it would be frustrating. And besides, he didn't want the hassle.

B. If clearances were sought and acquired, it would probably take a year to hire the special artists who alone could be entrusted to make such an "official copy." Surely, this American would not want to wait that long.

C. It could cost thousands of dollars, and this official is thinking, *That's more than I make in ten years! This American would never spend that much money!*

So, he uttered the word "impossible"! When I told him I had a wealthy donor who would pay "a very high price" and pressed him, I began to see a slow but certain change in attitude. "Well, it would take maybe two years!"

"That's okay."

Now, two years later, I have it! It stands a symbol to the "free spirit" and inspires pastors and believers who come for renewal.

It was *possible* after all!

Down with the word "Impossible!"

Remember: The subconscious lacks critical, intellectual capacities. It tends to believe anything fed into it, like a computer!

When uttered aloud, the word "impossible" is devastating in its effect on the subconscious. Thinking stops. Progress halts. Doors slam shut. Research comes to a screeching halt. Further experimentation is torpedoed. Projects are abandoned. Dreams are discarded. The brightest and the best of the creative brain cells nose-dive, clam up, hide out, cool down, and turn off in some dark but safe subterranean corner of the mind. By means of this defensive maneuver, the brain shelters itself against the painful sting of insulting disappointments, brutal, embarrassing rejections, and dashed hopes.

Now let someone utter the magic words, "It might be possible! I don't know *how,* or *when,* but it *might* be possible!" Those stirring words, with the siren appeal of a marshaling trumpet, penetrate into the subconscious tributaries of the mind, challenging and calling those proud powers to turn on and turn out! Buried dreams are resurrected. Sparks of fresh enthusiasm flicker, then burst into new flame. Tabled motions are brought back to the floor. Dusty files are reopened. Lights go on again in the long-darkened laboratories. Telephones start ringing. Computers light up. New budgets are revised and adopted. "Help Wanted" signs are hung out. Factories are retooled and reopened. New products appear. New markets open. The recession ends. A great new era of adventure, experimentation, expansion, and prosperity is born.[3]

You say, "But Dr. Schuller, you're quibbling about

---

[3]Schuller, *You Can Become,* 61.

words." And I answer emphatically, "Not so! I'm *not quibbling!* I'm *waging war* on dangerous, irresponsible, destructive forces that are released by seemingly intelligent and innocent remarks."

The real issue is *attitude*. Let someone get by with the judgment that something is "impossible," and a negative attitude toward progress, upward development, and creative breakthroughs will emerge. No! Let's scratch the word out of our vocabulary.

A cruel and insensitive critic once challenged me on my crusade to spread the idea that nothing is impossible. He was a cynic, one of the worst! He heard about my daughter's accident after which her left leg was amputated through the knee. "Anything's possible!? Come on, Schuller, you can't grow a new leg. That's impossible."

"Please," I said softly, "don't use that word. You may live to see the day when a "brain dead" person's heart, liver, eyes—yes, even legs—are transplanted!"

Impossible? You bet it's not in my dictionary! That's because "impossible" is a dangerous word!

Impossible? The word has the destructive power of an emotional thermonuclear bomb!

Impossible? That word is a knife thrust at the heart of creativity!

Impossible? That word is a roadblock to progress!

Let's unmask the word. We need to label these impossibilities correctly. They may be more honestly called:

- Prejudices!
- Challenges!
- Problems to be solved!
- Blind spots!
- Fatigue!
- Ignorance!
- Fear!
- Excuses!
- Ego problems!
- Laziness!

Call these "impossibilities" by their right name: *fears* that are taking over leadership in our thought processes.

They are the stubborn mental fences built by ignorance, apathy, or intolerance. Strip the mask from those "It's impossible's" and what do you find? A partial perception which produces illusion, which in turn produces confusion.

So! Let's expose those impossibilities for what they really are! Check, double-check, recheck your list of impossibilities before you give in to them:

• *It's Not Impossible!*

I just have to revise my plan. Rearrange my priorities. Remodel my blueprint. Redesign my strategy. Relocate my power center. Recheck my traditional answers. Get out of my rut!

• *It's Not Impossible!*

I just don't know how to do it, and I don't know anyone who does. I simply need to connect with smarter people. I must find someone who can invent new instruments or develop new procedures!

• *It's Not Impossible!*

I just have to solve some problems. I have to make some tough decisions; I need to set new goals. I may need to ask hostile persons for help. Am I prepared to turn my competitors into partners and my enemies into friends?

• *It's Not Impossible!*

I just need more time. It will take longer than I planned. I may have to cancel appointments to make more time. I'll have to streamline, remodel, and revise my calendar—or have other people help out when I can't find the time!

• *It's Not Impossible!*

I just need to raise more money, cut costs, eliminate waste, and set aside pet projects to release fresh financial resources. All I need are creative ideas, and money will flow to imaginative and resourceful efforts!

- *It's Not Impossible!*

I just have to think bigger! This will release a new burst of enthusiasm and energy. I must release my imagination from self-imposed, limited, too-small thinking.

- *It's Not Impossible!*

I just have to work harder. I must be willing to pay a higher price. I must increase my bid. I have to focus on whittling away what's restricting me. I can't "take it easy," or "be careful" and succeed!

- *It's Not Impossible!*

I just need more faith in myself, more self-confidence. I have to learn to manage my thinking, stop putting myself down, discard firmly fixed, locked-in negative distortions and preconceptions like: I'm too old; I'm not intelligent enough. I have to get in the habit of thinking, "I CAN."

- *It's Not Impossible!*

I just have to take charge—dare to begin. Decide to get started. Wrestle leadership from forces and faces that don't have my interests as their first concern!

- *It's Not Impossible!*

I just need a positive mental attitude. I have been reacting negatively. I will choose to believe that somehow, someway, sometime it might be possible.

- *It's Not Impossible!*

I just need more faith. I must learn to believe in tomorrow. I shall extricate my thinking from the repressive influence of past memories of failure and rejection.

- *It's Not Impossible!*

I just must never quit. All I need is patience that will never run dry. Soon traditional methods now ineffective will be replaced with new technological advances, and I'll be rewarded for my "never believe in never" attitude! I'll hold on. Tomorrow is replacing yesterday!

• *It's Not Impossible!*

I just need to tap into a higher power. There are sources of creative ideas I have yet to connect with; there are undiscovered forces waiting for me to discover and harness. So it's not impossible; I just can't do it alone. I need God's power! It's not impossible—if I'll have faith. Great things happen when man and God confront a mountain! I just have to Let Go and Let God.

• *It's Not Impossible!*

I just have to stop being so stubborn. I have to compromise on my silent stipulations, my unspoken demands, my unyielding set of givens. I have to have the wisdom to change my mind and the courage to declare it! I simply need to practice humility and doors will swing open! God will move in! Mountains will move! I will be blessed.

Once you've realized that it's NOT impossible, then you will be free to see the solutions! Then you can believe that there is a miracle around every corner. You can recognize that a *bend* in the road is not the *end* of the road!

Look around the corner! Keep going! Don't give up.

It Might Be Possible—If I Can Just Learn How to Do It!

What appeared impossible yesterday might be possible today! And what appears impossible today might be possible tomorrow! That's because every day new techniques are learned, new breakthroughs in technology are discovered.

Sadly, such a breakthrough in medicine came too late for the father of a friend of mine, Dr. Raymond Beckering. He was the minister who installed me in the ministry thirty-seven years ago, and he was the pastor who asked me to come from Chicago to California and begin a new church.

Dr. Beckering told me how his father died of diabetes

Impossibilities Vanish
When a Man
and His God
Confront a Mountain.

just one month before insulin was discovered. Had his father lived just thirty days longer, he probably could have added another twenty, thirty, maybe forty years to his lifetime.

I was reminded of how quickly change can occur when I spoke one day with John Templeton, the well-known investment counselor who was president of the trustees of Princeton Theological Seminary.

"Bob, do you realize how much change you and I have seen just in our lifetime?" John said. "In 1912, Americans had:

No income tax . . . no Federal Reserve.
No investment counselors . . . no mutual funds.
No vitamin tablets . . . no refrigerators.
No radios . . . no transcontinental telephones . . .
   no traffic lights.
No plastics . . . no man-made fibers . . . and no
   fluorescent lights.

"Much later after the 1929 boom, Americans still had:

No Social Security . . . no unemployment insurance.
No airmail . . . no airlines.
No Xerox . . . no air conditioning.
No antibiotics . . . no frozen foods.
No television . . . no transistors.
No lasers . . . and no nuclear energy.

"Who could have imagined back then the variety of new blessings in my lifetime, and who can imagine now the even greater new blessings in store for our children and our grandchildren?"

John continued, "We live in a world and a time of spiraling progress. We are better educated, better fed, and better housed than at any other time in the history of the world. Just look at how far we've come:

In 1912 Emil von Vehring produced an effective immunization against diphtheria and tetanus.

In 1921 Frederick Banting and Charles Best isolated the hormone insulin.

In 1928 Alexander Fleming discovered penicillin.

In 1929 Hans Berger developed the first electro-encephalograph.

In 1938 Max Theiler developed a vaccine for yellow fever.

In 1946 H. J. Muller received the Nobel Prize for Medicine for his research on x-ray-induced mutations.

In 1951 Andre Thomas developed the heart-lung machine.

The following year, Selman Waksman discovered streptomycin.

In 1954 Jonas Salk developed the first effective polio vaccine.

In 1967 Christian Barnard performed the first successful heart transplant in South Africa.

In 1982 Dr. William De Vries implanted the first permanent artifical heart in Barney Clark, in Salt Lake City.

In 1983 laser surgery became the method of choice for eye operations and the removal of spinal and brain tumors.

"More than half of the scientists who ever lived are alive today. More than half of the discoveries in the natural sciences have been made in this century. Discovery and invention have not stopped or even slowed down. Who can imagine what will be discovered if research continues to accelerate? Each discovery reveals new mysteries. The more we learn, the more we realize how ignorant we were in the past and how much more there still is to discover," John concluded.

You probably are not fully aware of your own strengths. Your net worth may actually have increased, your sphere of influence enlarged. Your network of friends may have actually grown. Things are possible or within the range of possibility to you today that would have been quite unthinkable not long ago.

When I think of how far we have come and how far we still have to go, I believe that anything is possible! In time we will learn the answers. In time we will discover the breakthroughs. In time we will see the impossible turned into the possible!

It Might Be Possible—If I Can Solve Some Problems!

The most impossible task you can ever imagine is never totally impossible—*if* you can just learn to solve some of the problems that are standing in your way.

I recently traveled by ship through the Panama Canal. I was looking forward to the experience, for I have always looked upon the canal as one of the world's great accomplishments.

The French tried for nineteen years to build it. They lost millions of dollars and hundreds of lives in the process. Eventually, they gave up the endeavor altogether. Then the Americans gave it a try. They decided that the solution was to create locks that would raise and lower the water level to let the ships pass. The accomplishment was incredible. It was a moving experience to ride a ship through that masterfully constructed canal.

Look at your impossibility as a problem that needs to be solved. If the problem appears too big, then you may need to break it up into several small problems.

Walter Burke was president of McDonnell Aircraft Corporation when President Kennedy called him and said, "We want to put a man on the moon."

Walter knew what was needed in order to make such an impossibility become a reality. He would need to develop a rocket booster big enough to release his spacecraft from gravitation. As an engineer, he learned that *a big problem was never one single problem.* So, the first thing he did was ask himself, "What are the different problems that altogether comprise the main problem?"

He carefully divided the problem up into about twenty problems. Of those problems he then decided which ones he could tackle himself, and which ones he would need help with, until he got to the point where there was only one problem left: the spacecraft that could defy gravity and go into orbit.

Walter said, "That's the happy phase. At that point I can focus all my energies on that one remaining problem, and when I focus everything on one problem I know it's just a matter of time before we can crack it!"

Well, of course, the rest is history. They solved the problems, and in 1969 Neil Armstrong became the first man to walk on the moon.

It Might Be Possible—If I Can Raise Some More Money!

Money is not the answer to all problems, but it is surprising how many problems are caused by lack of funds. Too many dreams are killed simply because of financial reports, and too many lives are ruined by bankruptcy.

So if you are tempted to give up and quit, ask yourself, "Would it be possible *if* I had enough money? What could I do *if* funds were not an issue?" It's amazing how someone with a Possibility Thinking passion can always come along and raise money when it's considered by experts to be "out of the question!"

Sybil Brand is one of the most remarkable women in Los Angeles County. Her offices are filled with awards. She is over eighty years old and considered one of the leading volunteers in America. She has served as the fund-raising chairman of the biggest fund raisers in California. In fact, Bob Hope once said about Sybil, "I can't do fund raisers anymore because Sybil's got 'em all."

Sybil got involved in volunteer services when she was five years old. The doorbell rang one day and Sybil answered it. The man standing there said, "Little girl, is your mother home?"

"Yes," answered little Sybil. She ran to her mother and said, "Momma, somebody wants to see you. He says he's hungry. Can't we give him our stove?"

That inauspicious start led to her tremendous work that

has earned her over two thousand awards. But she is most noted for her work with the Sybil Brand Institute in California. The institute is the county jail for women ages eighteen and older, which today houses over two thousand women.

Sybil happened to visit the jail one day and was horrified at overcrowded conditions. She decided to be a "doer" and became the driving force in raising a bond issue $8 million to build a jail. And she didn't stop there. She still goes to the jail to visit the women every three weeks and has a Christmas party for them every year. At that party she personally hands each inmate a Christmas gift.

The prisoners love Sybil. They hug her and write her letters thanking her. They call her "Lady Bountiful."

Through the years I have come to see that no one ever has a money problem. It is always an idea problem. There are always countless ways to come up with the money in a responsible, honest way.

It Might Be Possible—If I Can Think Bigger!

We all need to think bigger. I would dare to say that it is our limited thinking that creates many of our problems. So many "impossibilities" can be swept away when they are unmasked as just shortsightedness or limitations in our thinking.

All of us can learn from John and Greg Rice. They are twins. They are millionaries. They are famous. They are successful, happy, and fulfilled. All of this is nothing short of a miracle when you consider the fact that they are three feet tall and had obstacles other than their stature to overcome.

John and Greg were abandoned by their natural parents in the hospital when they were born. Then, when it was diagnosed that they would not be able to grow to full height, it took nine months for the state to find them a home that would accept both of them.

Fortunately, a wonderful, loving, Christian home was found. There the twins received the nurturing that would help them become the extraordinary men they are today.

John and Greg suffered another blow when their foster parents died while the boys were in the eleventh grade. Not long after that John and Greg got involved in real estate. Then they started speaking. In 1979 they were heard by staff members of the television program, "Real People." They were impressed by these two young men who were three feet tall, telling everybody else to think big.

They appeared on "Real People." Later they were in a television series. They continue today to be extremely successful on the international speaking circuit.

John once said to me, "Dr. Schuller, a lot of people look at Greg and me and say that we are lucky. We spell luck— W-O-R-K. We find that the harder we work, the luckier we get. You see, everybody, in one sense or another, is short in some area of his life.

"Some people like Greg and me are short of stature. Others are short of money. Most of us are short of experience. But, I think that perhaps the best example of a short person happened some three thousand years ago in Israel, when a teenager named David had it out with a Philistine bully named Goliath. Of course, you know the Bible says that David reached into his bag, took out a stone, slung it, and hit the giant on his forehead so that he fell face forward to the ground.

"But you know there are giants in our world that need slaying too, giants such as prejudice, negative thinking, lack of self-confidence, and self-pity. It may be like David; some of us don't think we have the proper ammunition to deal with the giants of our day, but I think all of us need to summon up our courage, reach deep within ourselves, pull out our stones, and hurl them toward the giants of our age. You see, it doesn't take much of a person to become a success. It just takes *all* the person has."

Greg added, "John and I could not have accomplished all that we have if it weren't for the strong religious foundation that our parents were able to instill in us. People look at us and say that we're a success. But John and I believe that the real secret of success is being happy—happy doing whatever it is you're doing. I think that John and I are probably two of the happiest people you'd ever meet because we don't look at our situation as being a problem."

John concluded, "You see, a lot of people make excuses for the situation they find themselves in. You have to take whatever situation that you are left with and make the most of it."

John and Greg have certainly made the most out of their situation. They are happy. They are not bitter. They are successful. Why? Because they have sent out a message of love, positive humor, and inspiration to millions of people. Is it any wonder that love, admiration, and other rewards should come back to them?

It Might Be Possible—If I Can Just Work Harder!

Louis Nizer, one of the greatest lawyers of the twentieth century, taught me the "magic" of another word. He said, "Every year I lecture to the law students at Yale and Harvard, and I always tell these students: I will teach you one word. That word will turn the dull mind into a bright mind. It will turn the bright mind into a brilliant mind. It will turn the brilliant person into a steadfast person. That word will open doors for you. That word will roll out red carpets for you. That word will connect you to some of the most beautiful and powerful people in the world. That word will give every person success. That miracle magic word is W-O-R-K!" A positive attitude toward work works wonders!

On one of my trips to Srinagar I ordered a gazebo. They had never heard of such a thing in this remote city between China and Pakistan.

"Impossible!" they said.

Nevertheless I sat down and drew the plans.

"Oh, we can do that!" they answered.

"What will it cost?" I asked.

The price they quoted seemed reasonable. "Will you take a personal check?"

Again, "Impossible!"

Just then I saw on the owner's desk a copy of *Time* magazine. It happened to be an issue with my picture in it. I picked up the magazine and showed him my picture. "You can trust me; I'm in here!" I said.

Wide-eyed, the woodworker read the story of the Beverly Sills concert that was held at the opening of the Cathedral. The article stated that even Frank Sinatra had bought a seat. "You know Frank Sinatra?" He was shocked. "I'll take your check!" he announced.

Eight months later the gazebo was delivered. Etched in the intricate carvings is the worker's name, his address—Srinagar, Kashmir, India—and then this quote, *"Our work is our worship."*

Anything is possible if you have a positive attitude toward work. Work will make the dream come true, and more often than not you will find that the work was fun! You enjoyed it! It didn't drain you—it revitalized you! You felt younger! Renewed! And most importantly it gave you a sense of accomplishment. You were proud of who you were and what you did. You committed yourself to your dream and, in the process, to God!

It Might Be Possible—If I Can Find Someone to Help Me!

Dr. Michael DeBakey is one of the most successful physicians living today. He will undoubtedly go down in the history books as one of the most innovative doctors in our generation. There isn't an operating room in the country that doesn't use instruments that bear the name "DeBakey" on them. And there isn't a hospital that doesn't have an intensive care unit.

The intensive care unit was started by Dr. Michael DeBakey in 1953. At that time there were great objections to it—not only by the doctors but also by the nurses.

Because there was a critical period immediately after the operation, he had to have highly trained personnel who were able to follow the patients closely. They had to be watched minute by minute, twenty-four hours a day. Fortunately, the administrator of the hospital agreed with Dr. DeBakey, and he set up the intensive care unit solely for his patients.

It was so successful that doctor after doctor began to say, "I'd like to have my patients in there too."

Consequently, over the next few years they had to expand the unit to take care of these other doctors and their patients. Interestingly enough, they forgot about their earlier objections. The intensive care unit became an integral part of the cardiac division of hospitals and soon spread to all wards of all hospitals in the country and even abroad.

"How many lives, how many human hearts have your hands held in your forty-plus years?" I asked him.

"Oh! Well over 50,000!" he answered.

When I heard that number, I was sure that he had to be exaggerating. Fifty thousand hearts seemed "impossible." But then Dr. DeBakey invited me to witness one of his surgeries. He led me into a viewing dome that hovered over four operating rooms, in which I could see four surgeries taking place simultaneously. A different team of nurses and doctors in each room worked on a surgical procedure. Supervising all four of these operations, floating from room to room, was Dr. DeBakey. I could see that 50,000 surgeries was hardly an exaggeration. If anything it was an understatement.

Later I expressed my amazement to him and my admiration for his ability to multiply his efforts through the help of others. He responded, "Well, I have an expression I often use in the operating room: 'If I just had a third hand I wouldn't need you at all.' But one of the reasons that we don't have a third hand is that God wants to keep us humble."

I asked him to explain how it felt to hold a human heart in his hand.

He said, "This is a God-given miracle. The heart is one of the most beautiful organs of the body. It's so very efficient. Just think of it beating away—sixty, seventy, or eighty times a minute for your lifetime, never getting tired unless there's some disease. Otherwise, it beats regularly and sustains your life. No wonder it's sometimes referred to as the seat of the soul.

"The fact is that you cannot help but feel this sort of Supreme Presence in the operating room. I think that if anyone doubts the existence of that spiritual Being, they should be in the operating room. You can't help but feel it very strongly. There's something about the sanctity of life when you're dealing with that very critical situation in the operating room. As far as heart surgery's concerned, you have to feel that there is another force there. And I've had that experience many times.

"I remember one patient who was supported on a heart-lung machine but the heart was not able to take over. Finally I reached the stage when it looked like I would have to give up. And then suddenly, for reasons that aren't clear at all, that heart started to beat again. All I could think was, 'Thank God.' I owed Him the credit. If He hadn't helped me through, the man would have died."

Dr. DeBakey has been able to share his expertise with thousands of people because he has surrounded himself with people—doctors and nurses—who are able to help him. He has also tapped into the Higher Source. Consequently, he has helped more people than most of us could ever dream of helping in a lifetime.

Are you frustrated at your lack of progress? Or do you feel you have reached the limits of your capabilities? Then maybe you need to reconsider the example of Dr. Michael DeBakey. Look for someone to help you. *Success might be possible* if you don't try to achieve it all by yourself!

It Might Be Possible—If I Realize That I Cannot Quit!

It takes courageous men and women to "keep on keeping on" when they run smack dab into failure or setbacks. It takes boldness to get up and run with the ball again after you've been tackled and had the wind knocked out of you.

It takes courage, it takes boldness, it takes integrity. I learned integrity on the Iowa farm. If you're born and raised on a farm, you develop instinctive integrity. You know that you have to milk the cows or the cows will dry up. If you plant corn, you know you're going to have to harvest it.

If you are familiar with the books *The Pursuit of Excellence* or *Passion for Excellence,* then you are acquainted with the name Stew Leonard. Stew is known as having the world's largest dairy store. And in 1986 he was chosen one of eleven people to receive the Presidential Award for Entrepreneurial Excellence.

Two months after Stew graduated from college his father died. Consequently, at twenty-one he was thrust into running the family business, delivering milk to private homes. Then customers started going to supermarkets. Stew felt like the iceman after the advent of refrigeration. The business was struggling when two men from the highway engineering department came and said they were going to level the dairy to make room for a new highway.

Stew didn't know what to do, so he asked his customers what their needs were, and they replied that they wanted fresh milk at the lowest price.

Stew had a dream. He dreamed of building a big store with a dairy right inside of it so the customers could come in and see their milk being bottled. He could save them money, and the children would have fun watching the operation through big windows.

When the new store was about three-quarters finished, the doubters arrived. They told Stew that he was crazy. They said it wouldn't work because people wouldn't make a special trip from the supermarket to come to his dairy store. They said that he would go broke. Stew told me later, "When the experts tell you that over and over again, you start to get down. My accountant told me that we were $100,000 over and that we were on the brink of going bankrupt. It was a tough time.

"The turning point of my life came one night when I couldn't sleep. I went downstairs and warmed up the coffee from supper. I sat there and I made two lists: one negative list of how I could fail and one positive list of how I hoped I could make it. The negative list was much longer. It was dark outside. It was raining, and I was down. I began to pray— not for God to solve all my problems, but to give me the courage and the strength.

"When the sun came up, my prayers were answered. My wife, Maryann, came downstairs. She said, 'Stew, what are you doing?'

" 'I'm worrying!' I said.

" 'Why?'

"And I replied, 'Because everybody's telling me we're going to fail. Everyone's telling me we're going to go broke.'

" 'Don't listen to those negative people,' she said. 'You're not going to go broke.' Then she went over to the kitchen desk drawer and took out a little passbook from the savings bank and said, 'Here's the $3,300 that we've inherited from my mother. I've had it put aside for the children's education. You can put that back after the new dairy's a success.'

"I felt so strong at that moment. My prayers had been answered. I just decided right then and there that I would make a go of it somehow. Surprisingly the experts were wrong, and the Possibility Thinkers, like Maryann, were right!"

I asked this dyanamic entrepreneur, "Stew, what do you think is the secret of your success?"

"Well, I believe that success is becoming yourself at your very best. It's nothing to do with someone else; it's to do with you. How are you compared to what you could be?"

When I visited his store, I asked him, "Stew, where are the cows? I'd like to milk a cow or two." Then I guess I gave him a little sermon about commitment, because two months later he came to visit me at the Crystal Cathedral. There in front of the congregation and a television audience of about three million, he presented me with a milk stool! And on this milk stool he had inscribed, "To Dr. Schuller, who once said, 'Quitting is never an option. The cows have to be milked come Hell or High Water.' "

When you've learned what commitment is all about—that quitting is never an option—then you will be free to see the possibilities!

It Might Be Possible—If I Get a New Attitude!

If you want to make your ideas work, you have to be in love with the dream. You have to desire it *passionately* with all your heart. When you are consumed by a passion and that passion has its tap root in a love for God and for human beings, then *the passion becomes compassion* and you will succeed.

Nobody understands this principle better than Marva Collins. Marva grew up in Atmore, Alabama, near Pensacola, Florida. Her parents instilled in her a strong desire to learn, be educated, and succeed. Today she is one of the most respected educators in the United States.

That is not an empty claim in view of the honors she has received. In 1981, along with Walter Cronkite, Supreme Court Justice Potter Stewart, and David Stockman, she was the recipient of the prestigious Jefferson Award for Great Public Service. And in 1982 she was honored as one of the legendary women of the world along with Beverly Sills, Nancy Kissinger, and Barbara Walters.

Marva Collins was offered the opportunity to be the Superintendent of the Los Angeles County School System. She turned it down. The President of the United States approached her and asked if she would be the Secretary of Education. She turned him down as well, because she is avidly pursuing her own dream.

Marva's dream is this: to tell teachers and children alike to believe in themselves. She promises her students, "I WILL NOT LET YOU FAIL!"

In 1974, after fourteen years of teaching in a big city school system, Marva quit because she was dismayed at seeing children pushed through a system where they were not learning. Armed with the $5,000 from her pension fund, she started a school that she called Westside Preparatory School. Westside Prep treats all students—black, white, wealthy, and welfare recipients—alike. Marva strives to instill self-esteem, self-determination, and pride in each child.

In the process she has transformed children who were labeled as retarded, troublesome, and truant into shining success stories. How does she do it? She starts by helping children to believe in themselves and in hard work. She believes that there is a candle of excellence within each child. Her technique is to rekindle that candle.

"Can't" is just another four-letter word. Its use is forbidden in Marva's school. Instead she teaches her students to believe that they CAN! The children believe and they succeed—time after time.

I recently had the chance to meet this remarkable woman and to learn more about her unique method of teaching. She said, "Dr. Schuller, with children in my hand, I have the ability to sculpt them into people who can become lifters rather than leaners. I have the ability to make these children greater than they ever thought they possibly could be. I can't describe for you how exciting it is to see the light that comes into a child's eyes when he begins to believe in himself."

"Marva," I asked her, "How do you do this? How do you teach children to believe in themselves?"

"Well, first of all, I always stayed out of the teachers' lounge because I would hear all of the doomsday cries about what the children could not do. I have never really seen a child that could not be reached. I believe that all children can achieve. The only thing that will keep a child from achieving is if we parents and teachers tell a child that he will not achieve."

"Are you saying that many children are being programmed to believe that they cannot succeed?"

"Unfortunately, in many cases, that is true. Let me give you an example. Last Thursday I went to a public school. I asked for forty-four children. I asked for the worst problems, the lowest achievers. There was one young lad who was standing in a corner. I said to him, 'You're far too handsome to stand in that corner with your back to me. I want to look at your handsome face.' I removed the child from the corner and I set him with the other children. Then I said to the children, 'Every time I reprimand you today and I ask you why aren't you going to do this, you will say, *Because I am too bright*.' Then I said to the young man, 'Why did I take you from the corner?'

"And he said, 'Because I am too bright.'

"I was in the classroom with these children for two hours, and as the time came for me to leave, they said with tears in their eyes, 'Please do not leave us. Can we go back to your school with you?'

"Many times our educators will have children write a hundred times, *I will behave in class.* At Westside Preparatory School we have a child stand up and give an impromptu talk on the theme, 'Why I am too bright to waste my time in class.'

"I teach my children to say *good-bye* to failure and *hello* to success!"

Marva Collins has learned the secret of success. She has learned that nothing is impossible if you program yourself to believe you can! If you eliminate the word *impossible* from your vocabulary, if you can reprogram yourself to think positively and to look for the possibilities, then you, too, will be able to say good-bye to failure and hello to success!

The right attitudes! They are fundamental. What we are after is nothing less than redeveloping, restructuring, human personality. It is not unlike developers who take over a slum district, level the rat-infested structures, clear the site, and lay the foundations for beautiful new high-rise structures in a parklike setting complete with flower gardens and green lawns.

So our first task is to clear the site by clearing from the mind old negative thought patterns and laying the underground foundations to support and sustain the new mental structures. The foundations we will lay are eight positive mental attitudes. Ready? Let's go!

CHAPTER 5

Turning Failure Thinkers into Success Thinkers!

*H*ow shall we get started on the success trip? Or start over after a terrible setback? (That's the right word, "setback," not "failure"!)

The answer to this question is another question: How do we go about our most important and our most urgent and our most difficult assignment, namely, turning our own—or someone else's—impossibility thinking into Possibility Thinking? Is it even possible? All of us have seen negative, dyed-in-the-wool, stubborn, and determined negative thinkers who resist all approaches, all therapies, and all suggestions that can turn their life around from the negative to the positive. Is it really possible to change someone from a "can't do" to a "can do" person?

Obviously, my answer to that question is predictable. My whole life's work has been built on the assumption that human nature can be radically transformed—turned inside out and upside down—and literally be born again! Jesus taught it. I believe it. My ministry is designed on this belief, and the results are impressive enough to convince me after a lifetime of concentrated efforts that people do change! Of this I am certain! My Possibility Thinking has benefited tens of thousands of persons who have responded to our therapy, whether in print or on the television screen. People who were programmed from infancy upward to be negative about their own potentiality have seen their frozen shells of resistance cracking under positive pressures. You bet it's possible!

Your number one job is to make certain that you are a Possibility Thinker! And don't count on a pep talk to do the job. Don't bank on a motivational rally or a "how to succeed book"—mine or anybody else's! These meaningful efforts may indeed set the tone, offer positive and pointed directions, even prepare the mental soil to get you going, but for results to be solid and lasting, nothing less than a psychological restructuring of the human personality must take place.

And to restructure a personality from negative to positive requires clearing the "construction site" of slum structures, the old negative attitudes, and laying new foundations that can support new skyscrapers.

So let's take a look at the blueprint that fits the Possibility Thinker. Think of this positive personality as a structure. What kinds of architectural blueprints are needed? What kind of a personality design are we after? What is the model that we can use and apply as a standard? And what are the foundation plans upon which a Possibility Thinking philosophy can be constructed?

If we took an attitudinal x-ray of the mental conditioning of a Possibility Thinker, we would see:

The eight positive mental attitudes of the Possibility Thinker

Obviously, a Possibility Thinker is someone who has practiced and is practicing a positive mental outlook. But can we dissect this positive mental attitude? Indeed, we can. For many years I've been observing and analyzing; I know that the design for the Possibility Thinking personality will call for a readiness to choose eight positive attitudes. Let's check them out.

I
Are You Ready to Choose a Positive Mental Attitude Toward CHANGE?

Here's what you can expect to hear from negative thinkers:

"Don't waste your time. They'll never change."

"I'm sorry; that's the way I've always been and that's the way I am. What you see is what you get!"

"You can't teach an old dog new tricks."

Note that these are *absolute*, not relative, observations. That's the hallmark of one who either (a) does not believe in change or (b) does not want to contemplate the prospect of change—for many reasons, some understandable and some barely tolerable.

On the other hand, Possibility Thinkers look upon change not as a threat but as the basis for hope! Where there is no possibility for change, there is no hope for improvement! Of course the unwillingness to have a positive attitude toward change is, more often than not, a subconscious defense mechanism of an insecure person, who often sees himself as the victim of change. The inwardly secure person sees himself as the creator of changes that require plans and preparation before tomorrow comes! Of the grand collection of positive attitudes, this positive attitude toward progress is the most basic.

A positive attitude toward change also requires humility. Only the self-assured person dares to be humble, for humility demands that we be willing to admit that we do not know all the answers and that some of our answers are wrong.

Obviously, a variety of proposals we encounter will instantly be judged to be "hopelessly impossible" based upon the knowledge possessed at a given time. But the Possibility Thinker assumes that if the proposal has within itself seeds of creativity, then it deserves sincere attention and honest research. Can you see how the Possibility Thinker is thinking in relative instead of absolute terms? Can you see how there is an underlying willingness to change conclusions based upon the assumption that the person has been programmed with some errors, falsehoods, and inaccuracies?

We will never know how many people have failed because they were programmed with errors and never challenged their own flawed and faulted opinions, some of which needed to be amended, updated, revised, or rejected!

II
Are You Ready to Choose a Positive Mental Attitude Toward YOURSELF?

Because you have a positive attitude toward change, it's possible for you, a Possibility Thinker, to have a positive mental attitude toward yourself.

You can look at your limitations and believe that they can be corrected or supplemented.

You can look at your faults and shortcomings and believe that you can improve yourself.

You can look at your inadequate experience and training and believe that you can acquire new skills.

You can look at your fears and build pillars of courageous faith into your life. You can say, "God plus me equals a majority."

You can look at your imperfections and respect yourself anyway; you can affirm to yourself, "When I'm good—I'm good; when I'm not—I'm human!"

When I first wrote my flagship book on Possibility Thinking, *Move Ahead With Possibility Thinking,* I felt I had dealt with success in such a way that people could move from low achievement to high achievement. But I found that there was a major weakness in the book. My assumption had been that the readers would approach the subject with a positive self-image. But I heard from readers who expressed such negative self-images that I realized another book was necessary. I followed with *Self Love, The Dynamic Force of Suc-*

cess. I observed that Possibility Thinking cannot exist in a personality unless that person values himself highly and believes in what he can be. The "I am" will determine the "I can." "The me I see is the me I'll be." If we want to design a blueprint for a Possibility Thinking personality, the outline must include a positive self-image.

Now, attaining a positive self-image is not easy, for society does not tend to pat us on the back. Tragically, the family often fails as well. Faults are highlighted. Mistakes and sins are underlined! Criticism and condemnation immediately and instinctively come to the fore, while honest compliments get short shrift. Even education has failed to do the job. Religion, too, is not without its faults on this score. Only God knows how many persons have been programmed from childhood upward to believe negatively about their own talents and abilities.

We, all the while, tend to be our own worst enemies. We are reticent to accept compliments. Praise tends to embarrass us. Accolades are appreciated, but we really don't know how to accept them. So we resist the programming that would strengthen our healthy, positive pride.

At the same time we have a natural, normal inclination to exaggerate our shortcomings. Within our subconscious, which is well described as a supercomputer, a vast collection of negative programming stunts our budding self-confidence. Massive reprogramming may need to take place. For this reason my ministry has made a disciplined commitment always to be positive in presenting Christianity.

"Why don't you tell people what sinners they are?" I'm often asked.

The answer is obvious. People have no trouble believing they're sinners. That's easy. The most difficult task is to help people believe how beautiful they can become if they will allow the love of Christ to fill their lives! Constant positive reinforcement is an unending need. People need to be told daily, "I am God's idea—so I must be okay."

Possibility Thinkers are those persons who intuitively embrace a positive self-image and assume that they "can."

It has been said that because of its body shape and the

size of its wings the bumble bee is an aerodynamic impossibility, but it flies anyway because it has never been told it can't!

Walter Anderson, editor of *Parade* magazine—probably the most widely read weekly periodical in the United States with an estimated sixty million readers—confided in me that he received straight A's in college because "I was offered this scholarship and I mistakenly assumed that if I didn't get straight A's I would lose the scholarship. Therefore I worked hard and got all A's!"

Now what does that say about human potential? Nobody told Walter Anderson that it was not possible to get straight A's! So he did. He felt he had to!

One of the longest sermon titles I've ever used was "I didn't know how heavy my luggage was until I stopped carrying it." In this message I mentioned how I always had insisted on carrying my own bags at airports. I would have felt weak and old and infirm if I had accepted my hosts' offer to help. One day I accepted the offer. With both hands completely free I was able to gesture while I walked and talked. I could even shake hands with friends whom I met at the airport or oblige someone with an autograph or a hug! Suddenly I realized how heavy my baggage had been.

How much baggage of negative attitudes toward ourselves have we been carrying along with us? Let it go! Drop it! Abandon these self-condemning and self-belittling opinions!

Failure is never final to the person who has a healthy self-regard. Success is never ending to the person who keeps believing, "I've got a lot to offer and I've still got a lot to give. Next time I'll make it!"

III
Are You Ready to Choose a Positive Mental Attitude Toward LEADERSHIP?

The Possibility Thinker has an extraordinarily positive mental attitude toward leadership. Because he values his own intelligence and ability and his own instinctive and intuitive

qualifications, he now experiences a profound inner awareness that he can instigate change in his own life and in the
world around him! This awareness is the birth of leadership. For leadership is the marvelous consciousness that
says:

- I can sort out the alternatives, I can list the options, I
  can review all of the possibilities, and I can make the
  choice!
- I will decide which option, alternative, and possibility
  should be my goal.
- I have the responsibility to make decisions!
- I will be responsible for my own destiny!
- I am a person, not a puppet! I am far more than a
  "supercomputer"! I am a moral creature. I have a will.
  I can make judgments. This is what being a human
  being is all about! And as soon as I sense that this is
  what leadership is all about, then I will think for my-
  self!
- I will change what needs to be changed within my
  mental and emotional programming.
- I will not surrender leadership to other faces or forces.
- I will not abdicate my decision-making responsibility
  to negative thoughts. Rather—I will choose to put my
  own positive thoughts in command!
- I will rise to the top! I will be the leader of my own life.
  I will not fear or shrink from this awesome and es-
  teemed position of power.
- I will remain the captain of my soul! I will not step
  aside from the helm and allow others to take the leadership role over my own body, mind, and eternal soul!

The Possibility Thinker asks, "Where will I be five years,
ten years, twenty years from now?" and answers, "That depends on the decisions I make today and the goals I choose as
a leader of my own destiny."

IV
Are You Ready to Choose
a Positive Mental Attitude Toward PROBLEMS?

You can begin to see it emerge already, can't you? The skeletal structure of the successful achiever! Of course this person has a positive mental attitude toward change and can turn tough times around. Tomorrows can be changed until they shine brilliantly. The Possibility Thinker has a positive attitude toward himself, which produces a positive mental attitude toward leadership. The success-oriented individual can assume leadership over his own destiny and does not have to abdicate responsibility as a human being to anyone.

The result is a personality that has *a positive mental attitude toward problems.* Without this quality, goals will never be set because the person will suspect intuitively that goals will produce problems. And that's right! And if a positive self-image is lacking, so will be the confidence that problems can be solved or managed creatively.

Show me a person with a positive mental attitude toward personal problem solving and we are well on our way toward shaping the Possibility Thinking personality that's going to succeed. No doubt about it!

Without a positive mental attitude toward problems, a person will never make the personality shift from the impossibility thinking posture to the Possibility Thinking posture.

Good news! This switch in attitude, which is so basic and fundamental, is teachable! People can learn a positive mental attitude toward problems! And at this point we frequently see the beginning of a personality transformation from the negative to the positive! Let's see what happens when we have a positive mental attitude toward problems.

How Possibility Thinkers Perceive Problems

1. To begin with, problems are okay. They are not sinful. We don't need to be ashamed of them. Our self-esteem does not need to be battered or tarnished because we face problems. They are natural—in fact, inevitable if we are growing!

All growth produces problems. In my early days as a pastor I did a great deal of marriage counseling. When couples would confide in me about their conflicts, they frequently showed embarrassment. It was almost as if they thought they were abnormal! At the moment of their wedding, all was so blissful and beautiful. Somehow, at some time, difficulties arose, even though they were not exactly sure why or by whom the troubles developed.

My first tactic was always to tell them, "That's okay; don't be ashamed or embarrassed. It's quite natural. Remember, even though interpersonal relationships may be operating on a level of exceptional harmony and happy rhythm, each person in the relationship is still growing at his or her own rate. So don't be surprised if the gears don't mesh perfectly when one grows faster than the other." I would often remove my wristwatch, hold it up, and explain, "This wristwatch can be created with precision engineering. Each gear will flawlessly match the intersecting gear. Every moving part is carefully designed and crafted to fit perfectly in the whole scheme of rhythmic harmony. Put it all together. Wind it up. And you can expect trouble-free operation for a long, long time. But suppose each gear was a living organ, independent while it is interdependent! And let's suppose each moving part of this watch was growing at a different rate than the neighboring wheels. How long could this watch run before it stopped and became hopelessly deadlocked in a nonnegotiable and irreconcilable jam?

"Be of good cheer! Relationships between persons need constant tuning and alignment. So relax. Do not be humiliated. Wake up and join the human race. Problems are okay! They only prove that you are living and growing and very human!"

Begin with this logical concept and you will be spared shame and remain free to move into the realm where your self-esteem is still intact. And with that support you can move on and discover creative solutions to these natural problems.

2. Possibility Thinkers realize they have created their own problems. Now that your self-esteem is intact, you need to protect yourself from a natural and normal inclination to self-pity by understanding that *you have created your own problems.*

Marital difficulties? We created problems when we married! Business problems? Well, if we hadn't chosen to go into business in the first place, we wouldn't have problems, right? When we Possibility Thinkers analyze our problems, we understand that we really created them when we set the goals, made the decisions, and signed our names to meaningful commitments. Once we accept this, we are taking a positive rather than a negative attitude toward our condition. The impossibility thinker instinctively, intuitively, impetuously, and impulsively tends to blame others for his frustrating predicaments. He falls easy prey to "victimitis."

"Life isn't fair."

"I got a raw deal."

"No one understands what I have to put up with."

And so the negative mental attitudes toward problems only exacerbate the problems!

When I reached my daughter's side after her leg had been amputated, I said to her, "Carol, your biggest problem may be to fight the tendency toward self-pity." She snapped back, "Don't worry about that, Dad, I've got enough problems without *choosing* that one!" She had created her own problem when she made a decision to accept her cousin's invitation to hop on the back of his bike and take a spin down the road.

Can you see what's happening? The person who faces problems is spared from the tendency to become defensive, which will really make matters worse! The negative person becomes defensive and fails to hear and listen to the constructive guidance and helpful advice that are being offered. A person who accepts responsibility for personal problems, on the other hand, can begin to take corrective action and will emerge from the crisis wiser, smarter, and stronger—and go on to greater successes.

Always remember: "Failures" are only problems waiting to be solved!

3. No problem is ever "a" problem. A problem is really a collection of a couple, a few, or many problems. Are you unemployed? Well that problem is a collection of several problems. You may lack training and skills in the jobs that are in demand. You may lack the financial capability to give yourself the specialized education required for today's job market, which probably means you are not connected to persons who could provide scholarships. Another part of the problem may be that you don't know where such training is offered—at a lower cost than you might have imagined.

You must carefully approach every problem with a positive mental attitude and with the assumption that the problem combines several complexities. Break it apart. Tackle each problem separately. Work on the easy ones first. Remember when you were taking an exam in high school or college? The first thing you did was answer the simple questions. That gave you the confidence that you could pass the test, right? Possibility Thinkers may solve the problem of seeking new employment by dividing the difficulty: "I have to move from my current place of residence. . . . I have to take advance training. . . . I have to meet the right people."

As you divide, you will conquer. That's the classic strategy of winning any battle!

4. Every problem has its match—somewhere! There's a miracle to match every mountain. I may not know how to solve my problem, but someone does. "There's someone, somewhere, who can help me understand my problem and guide me on how I can deal with it; therefore I have no reason to be discouraged" is the distinctive attitude of the Possibility Thinker. No wonder success keeps moving along and failures are only temporary setbacks!

5. Every problem is intrinsically and inherently pregnant with some positive possibility. The attitude of the Possibility Thinker is: "*No problem is without positive value.*" I am writing this particular chapter only days after returning from a lecture tour that took me from one end of the Japanese islands to the other. I was particularly impressed with one corporate chief whose business had been hit by a recession. His company's market share on the international scene has diminished sharply. His attitude? It is beautiful! He summed it up to his top corporate officers: "We're facing more serious problems than ever before. And that's wonderful. For problems in an organization are like pain in the body. They are nature's way of blessing us with a wonderful warning that we need to make changes."

So a problem is viewed as a possibility. The obstacle is perceived as a potential opportunity. The scar can be turned into a star. We will be able to reap dividends from our difficulties. We'll turn these frustrations into fruitful experiences. The problem? It is an opportunity to spot a weakness in the system. That's important and valuable information!

The market pressures shift, the needs of people change, and the problem leads us to wisdom, as certainly as if it had come out of our own research and development laboratory! We will now discover new and vital needs and redesign our goals to meet them. We'll look back and thank the problem for nudging us into a more successful strategy. And so our success will be unending! Thank God for problems!

6. *Every problem is now perceived as either (a) solvable, or (b) manageable, or (c) exploitable.* We're spared from despair. We are immune to pessimism, and our optimistic outlook remains healthy. This problem will be dissected and dealt with constructively and redemptively, which means we're going to solve it! If we don't solve it, at least we will manage it by controlling its negative impact on us. And if we control the potential damage or actual ill effect upon us as individuals or institutions, we will have an opportunity to practice crisis management. That will be another feather in our cap! Any person can be successful on smooth seas. How much more meaningful the victory will be if the battle has been difficult.

So it is a choice: I will either let the problem manage

me—or I will manage the problem. So long as I choose not to surrender to discouragement, depression, and final despair, I will have proven myself to be bigger than my mountain! And I can be absolutely positive about one factor in the whole problem-solving scene: "I can choose how I will react to what happens to me." As a result, self-respect and self-esteem will come out shining like a full moon on a silvery sea! I will earn and receive the respect of respectable people!

While writing this chapter I watched one of America's great leaders declare personal and corporate bankruptcy. The ex-governor of Texas, John Connally, whose business assets once approached $500 million, saw his business deteriorate as oil prices fell. He was being interviewed on a national morning television show about his move to the bankruptcy courts. He looked the TV audience straight in the eye: "Oil prices fell. There was nothing we could do about it. We had leveraged our assets. We watched the assets rapidly lose value until they failed to match our liabilities. We went to Hong Kong and to the markets of the world to refinance our operations, quite confident that with the passing of time values would rise again and we would once more be solvent. But we failed. We were left with no recourse but to seek the legal protection of the courts through bankruptcy."

I watched the ex-governor of Texas explain his position with integrity, and I was profoundly impressed! There was no evidence of "victimitis." There was no self-pity. It was a forthright report of a businessman who realistically had watched the economy shift, leaving him without the financial base that had been his only a few years before.

"I'll be selling our silver. We have, of course, sold our horses. We will liquidate our personal property to try to pay off as many of the creditors as possible," he explained calmly. His poise in the face of this predicament drew immense respect from me.

When every other element of a problem is out of your control, remember you can still manage your reaction!

When you choose a positive emotional reaction to your

unsolvable problem, you have managed your problem—at the bottom line!

7. *Every problem is temporary.* Possibility Thinkers know that tough times never last but tough people do. Every problem has its peak, and then it's downhill all the way. Every valley has its low point. Reach it and there's only one way to go from that point, and that's upward. Problems are not eternal; they are temporal. With this positive attitude toward the transitory nature of every human difficulty, it's possible to keep a sensible and successful positive mental attitude through the dark and stormy periods!

He was so depressed, he threatened suicide. "Suicide is a superdumb reaction," I reminded him. "For sucide is a permanent solution to a temporary problem!"

The storms are always the losers to the sun. The sunrise always overtakes the night. Winter always loses to Spring.

8. *The Possibility Thinker's attitude toward problems is that "They are distortions as I perceive them today."* I am exaggerating the enormity of the problem. I am probably exaggerating the problem's negative impact on me because I am under stress. According to the predictable human behavioral responses, I am overreacting to this problem's negative effect on my today and my tomorrows. Therefore, I shall be suspicious of my perceptions of the power of my own problems—and remind myself that this is not nearly as serious as I think it is.

The worst that could happen is something that has been faced by people with far fewer emotional, spiritual, and other human resources than I possess. They survived. So will I! And I shall be a wiser and better person when it's all over.

9. *Most problems are not problems after all.* That's the first distortion that was clarified in my mind. I called them problems, but they were only decisions waiting to be made. And as soon as I realized this, I moved back to my positive attitude toward myself, toward my leadership capabilities, and

toward change. So now I am prepared and poised to make some tough, difficult, and, yes, painful decisions. But once I have made them, my "problems" will be gone!

10. *Finally, no impossible problem is* totally *impossible.* This is the final conceptual ingredient of the Possibility Thinker's positive mental attitude toward problems. When faced with a problem that others call totally impossible, the Possibility Thinker counters with a wise proclamation: "No impossible problem is ever totally impossible." There is always something I can do about some aspect of this problem. I will call upon my God to give me the wisdom to see what part of it is within my abilities to handle, and I will deal with that. More often than not I will be shocked and surprised to find that dealing with that one seemingly insignificant aspect in the complexities of my problem turned the tide. A breakthrough awaited me. New forces and sources from "out of the blue" rescued me, all because I had the attitude that even though I couldn't save the entire ship, I could save a life or two. Now you can see how a positive mental attitude toward a problem puts truth in the promise: "Success is never ending; failure is never final."

V
Are You Ready to Choose a
Positive Mental Attitude Toward PEOPLE?

I have asked innumerable successful leaders, "What's the secret of your success?"

Invariably the answer has been the same: "Good people that work for me."

I have also interviewed dozens of persons who were leading institutions that were going downhill—"What went wrong? What's been your biggest problem?"

Once again, their answers were the same: "Ineffective people!"

How do we translate this? It means that successful people have a positive mental attitude toward people! They believe the best about people and extract the best from people!

Of course, they don't bat a thousand. But the person who has a negative attitude about people will not dare delegate to anyone: "I don't believe they can do a good enough job"; or "They'll get all the credit, and I will have to take the risk and do the work"; or "They'll just rip me off for what they can get out of me and then leave me stranded. I'll just do it myself! I'll pull it off all alone. I'll do it my way and do it right."

In *The Be-Happy Attitudes* I noted that the number one attitude for happiness is drawn from the words of Jesus: "Blessed are the poor in spirit,/For theirs is the kingdom of heaven" (Matt. 5:3). What does this mean? It means that we should have the attitude that "I am impoverished if I feel that I have to go it alone in life. I need help. I can't do it alone." That's what this beatitude means. And it is the starting point of true success! For the "people who need people are in fact the luckiest people in the world"!

"I can do all things—*through Christ* who strengthens me." And how does Christ strengthen us? Does He come here with meat and bones and hair and blood to stand at our side? Yes, He does. For His spirit enters into human beings whose lives He controls positively. So when I listen to the advice of smarter people, Christ strengthens me. When I accept help from people who can do a better job than I can, Christ strengthens me. I seek the counsel of experts in law, finance, taxes, and marketing. They are good people, smart people, tough people in whose lives Christ is living to be my strength!

This means I will not be defensive under constructive criticism from good counsel. This may be Christ coming to correct me! I will have the attitude that some people are smarter than I am; I will have the attitude that some people know something that I don't; I will have the attitude that there are people who are more skillful and gifted and creative than I am. So I shall be open to them, rather than closing my mind and my life to the contributions they can make.

What's happening here is that I am preventing personal ego problems from blocking healthy and constructive relationships with good people who could make the difference between my disastrous failure or my glorious success! The

person who has such a positive mental attitude toward people inspires them to contribute their best loyally and successfully. In other words, people who believe in people are
more often than not abundantly rewarded!

Have you wished that people would trust you? Believe
in your ideas? Accept the wisdom and advice that you could
bring into their limited awareness? And when your help was
accepted, did you not pour it out generously and enthusiastically? Of course! No wonder Possibility Thinkers succeed. Success or failure is going to be determined by the
people we attract. We will attract people who will lead us to
success if we trust them, believe in them, and listen to them!
It's that simple. And if you don't believe it, check the alternative. Consider the negative approach, and you will see a
lonely man who knows it all and is headed for failure. If by
any chance he pulls it off alone, he'll be a lonely person. Who
likes to eat dinner alone? Success without social respect can
be ultimate and dismal failure!

The saddest funeral I ever conducted as a pastor was for
a wealthy man who had not a single mourner at his funeral!
His three adult sons lived in the community but did not at-
tend. I have never had an experience like it before or since.
Only the mortician and I were there! When I asked for an
explanation, the funeral director said, "All he wanted was to
make more money and acquire his selfish toys. He didn't
have time for his children. He had no time for his wife. He
had no time or money to share with the church or the social
charities. He hit it lucky in the stock market! But he died an
extremely sick and lonely man. In fact the doctors say his
loneliness brought on his early death!"

That's failure!

VI
Are You Ready to Choose
a Positive Mental Attitude Toward
EMOTIONAL WELL-BEING?

The Possibility Thinker has a positive mental attitude
toward the mood swings that come and go in his life. He

understands that his emotional enthusiasm demands rest periods at times. He can't be "high" all the time! The Possibility Thinker recognizes this and hence is not frightened by a "down mood." Rather, he says, "Well, I'm going into a time of emotional retreat. This is a phase of emotional intake. I shall wait on the Lord and He will strengthen my heart. I shall not be afraid or unduly anxious about these moods that would lower my spirits."

Mind you, not all negative emotions are destructive. . . . For example—

> "Sweet sorrow"—When saying farewell.
> "Happy sadness"—When recalling bygone days.
> "Healing grief"—When weeping at a funeral.
> "Righteous anger"—When facing horrific injustice.
> "Constructive Fear"—When quitting smoking or
> some other harmful habit.
> "Corrective Guilt"—When needing to get back on
> track.

Negative emotions can be constructive.

What's important is that I control my moods to make me a better person. Am I for a brief moment discouraged? Well, I'm not going to surrender to this mood. And it will pass.

"I'm really hurting, but I'm going to bounce back" is another positive attitude highlighted in my book *The Be-Happy Attitudes*. No wonder Possibility Thinkers make it. They realize that low times are understandable, often inevitable, and sometimes even helpful. What's important is how we handle them.

Specifically, we never make negative, irreversible decisions in a down time! This is one time when the decision not to make a decision is a positive decision! For it proves that we are still in control of our moods.

Amazingly, the mood shifts. The positive feelings always return! They will inevitably come to put sunshine back into our lives! You, the Possibility Thinker, are well aware of the fact that you have had many good days since you were born. There may be a few or many negative memories, but you look at your life positively and know there have been many, many happy times. And these good times will bubble into consciousness again and again in the form of unpredictable, unexpected, but joyously welcomed moods of fresh delight! A melody in the background will provoke a memory of a happy time, and you will start whistling again.

We can see how important this positive mental attitude toward moods is in the whole success process! Without it a person surrenders at a weak time to a down thought and predictably nose-dives to a crash landing! Instead of this, the positive-mental-attitude person does nothing but simply wait and think, and think some more.

In our busy world we don't take time enough to think. An experienced commercial pilot sat with me one day on a transcontinental flight. "Did you ever have any problems or crises? And how did you handle them?" I asked.

"Oh, yes," he said, "I've had a few. But when I was a pilot in the military, I learned 'In a potentially catastrophic emergency, don't do anything! Just think! Don't touch a single control! *But think!*'"

He continued, "I was in the group that had the task of bombing Tokyo Bay during World War II. In a dive preparing to drop my bomb load, I was hit by incoming fire. I thought for a moment that I was finished. But I did nothing! I can't tell you how difficult it was to resist grabbing the controls. All I did was think, and my thoughts were, *I believe I'm on a correct pattern. I'll come out of this.* And in fact the controls were set for me to come out of the dive, and I did. Had I done anything at all to throw the control pattern off, I would have been finished!"

So when your moods take a nose dive, don't do anything—just think! And wait! And of course fill your mind with prayer and positive thoughts. You will master your moods. And it will make the difference between success and failure—believe me!

Oh, how hard it is to resist the temptation to lunge into action when you have run into disaster. Yet, the first step to survival is this: DO NOTHING!

Fred Markwell, a seaman from Australia, teaches this advice in a survival manual that he has written. And Markwell is certainly an authority, having survived a gale in the waters off Australia with fifteen- to thirty-foot waves crashing about him for seven hours.

Markwell was skipper of a luxury launch, the *Nocturn*, that carried four passengers. Despite a peaceful forecast, a sudden storm blew up. Markwell could tell by its fierce intensity that they were in severe danger. He and the four passengers donned bright orange jackets to attract help, should they need it. He also stocked the dinghy with flares.

When the *Nocturn* began to pull apart, Markwell and the passengers climbed over the side, into the dinghy, but it was immediately swamped by an engulfing wave and the passengers were dumped into the water. Pieces of the *Nocturn* floated past Markwell. He spotted a piece of pine only two feet by nine inches. He rested his head on the splinter of wood and said to himself, "Don't use your energy. You'll need it. Do nothing you don't have to do!"

Then he spotted the wooden frame of a divan that had been stripped of its upholstery. It was about forty yards away. He was tempted to swim with all his might and clamber aboard to safety. But he talked himself out of such a rash and deadly course of action. Instead he waited until a wave came and then rode the wave, using the piece of pine to keep his head up. Another wave brought him to within a few feet of the divan, and the temptation to swim to it was almost unbearable. But he stopped himself and continued to "surf" until he was within easy reach of the frame.

Once on the frame, Fred Markwell forced himself to get some rest. He closed his eyes. Although he didn't sleep, the rest gave him the strength to survive the chilling hours that he had to wait for rescuers to find him.

Seven hours after the *Nocturn* went down, Fred Markwell and two passengers who had clung to the side of the dinghy were rescued by a helicopter search team. Two of the passengers had drowned.

Markwell says that survival in the water in a gale is possible if you keep hold of yourself. *"One constructive thought is worth an hour of flapping around in futility,"* he said.[1]

All the while, the positive mental attitude toward emotional well-being makes the person sensitive to the differences between negative and positive feelings. The Possibility Thinker gradually gains the ability to recognize and reject negative feelings, then intuitively and self-consciously senses and submits to the positive feelings! All forms of emotional input—relationships, books, magazines, religious teachings, lectures—affect our emotional well-being for better or worse. We begin to sense whether our thoughts and experiences are giving us joy, hope, confidence, courage, love. If these positive emotions are stimulated, we allow ourselves to remain in the groove. But if ideas, individuals, institutions, activities, or experiences tend to leave us with negative feelings (discouragement, depression, anger, guilt, shame), we take *immediate* corrective action to extract ourselves or, if this is not practical, create shields to protect ourselves from negative impact. My own shields are prayer and Bible verses.

There are times when the summer conditions seem to multiply the insects in our garden at home. In the balmy night I want my wife to join me in taking a stroll through the garden. There was a time when her answer was, "I'm not going to go out and get bitten by the mosquitoes."

"But you'll miss the fragrance of the jasmine in the evening," I would say.

There are times when I realize I must endure negative vibrations. Anxiety? Fear? Worry? Frustration? Anger? These negative emotions are uninvited, unwelcomed, and brief seatmates as I make my bus trip through this life. But I do not stop living. I press on after I have developed an emotional shield to neutralize the negatives. I thereby do not allow them to penetrate the core of my personality!

There are times, too, when we have to work with people who are negative and extremely difficult to love. How do we handle these experiences? Again, we simply create emotional shields for the stressful times. For me this is a constant busi-

---

[1] *Los Angeles Times*, Nov. 23, 1979.

ness of praying positive prayers. I call upon the Holy Spirit for His love power to fill me with patience and the power to rise above the negative experiences, exactly the way a jetliner rises above the storms by climbing higher.

A positive mental attitude toward emotional well-being cultivates in the Possibility Thinker's mind a sharpened sensitivity to the emotional value of words. We need to listen and hear whether words are positive or negative in the feelings that they generate. Words like "never" are immediately suspect to those with a positive mental attitude. They know that the word "impossible" will drain out positive emotions and open the floodgates for negative feelings.

Dr. Smiley Blanton once brought mental healing to a depressed person by prescribing that this patient eliminate the words "if only" out of his vocabulary, substituting instead the words "next time." That simple, therapeutic technique worked wonders!

Likewise, I have been telling people to scratch the word "just" out of their vocabulary when it applies to their own person or position. "Just" a wife. "Just" a homemaker. "Just" a layperson. "Just" a student. "Just" a truckdriver. "Just" a salesman. "Just" an employee. In all of these instances the word "just" robs persons of the proper pride they should have in their positions.

I'll never forget the time that Doris Day admonished me for using the word "lost" as it related to her late husband. She made me aware of its negativity. It strikes the subconscious, which lacks judgment capabilities, and immediately registers negative feelings.

Likewise, Dr. Daniel K. Poling said to me when I wrote a sympathy letter to him after his wife passed away, "She's not lost; I know where I can find her." Now that's a fantastic understanding of the emotional weight and worth of the right words!

By maintaining a positive mental attitude toward my emotional well-being, I clear my mind for a creative mental state which is receptive to creative ideas. Fuming and fretting create tension, which blocks creative thinking. So a positive mental attitude toward emotional well-being immediately frees my mind to receive new, creative, redemptive, and success-producing ideas!

VII
Are You Ready to Choose a Positive Mental Attitude Toward CREATIVE IDEAS?

The Possibility Thinker has a profound reverence and respect for his own thoughts. He's well aware of these facts:

Nobody has a money problem; it's always an idea problem. The right idea always will attract the money.

Nobody has a time-management problem; it's an idea-management problem first and foremost!

On the other hand the *im*possibilty thinker allows ideas to come and go through his mind carelessly and frivolously. A casual, cavalier attitude toward thoughts is characteristic of the negative thinker. He hasn't developed a positive mental attitude toward the power of positive ideas.

By contrast the Possibility Thinker knows that one idea can create a whole new industry. One seemingly simple thought can lead to the invention of a product that can change the lifestyle of millions. Ideas are viewed with the same value that a farmer looks upon a seed.

Good ideas should never be rejected with the time-worn excuses that negative thinkers automatically rattle off. I have for the past twenty years been sifting, sorting out, and cataloging the most widely-used excuses used by impossibility thinkers when they reject possibility-pregnant ideas.

1. "It can't be done."
2. "It's out of the question."
3. "We simply don't have what it takes to do it."
4. "It's too risky."
5. "I just don't like it!"
6. "We're too late; somebody else is already doing it."
7. "But nobody is doing it. I don't want to be the odd duck!

8. "We've got enough problems on our hands already."
9. "We're doing fine as it is."
10. "But the forecast would lead us to believe. . . ."

How many other excuses are frivolously and foolishly presented to abort ideas that contain seeds of positive potential?

By contrast Possibility Thinkers face the same "excuses" and turn them into opportunities. This doesn't mean they plunge ahead recklessly, irresponsibly, and without adequate research and preparation. No, they ask questions to determine the validity of the budding idea. Possibility Thinkers will ask basic questions like:

1. "Does anybody need it?" They know that the secret of success is to find a need and fill it.
2. "If nobody is doing anything about it, why not? And if somebody is doing something about it, could we do it better and cheaper?"
3. "Is it newsworthy? If we tackled it, could we attract good attention to ourselves?" They know very well that however great a product may be, potential customers must know it's available. And if it's a new product or a better product, it may get free advertising by making news!
4. "Does this idea fit into our company image? If not, should we set up a new corporation to deal with it?"
5. "Is there some way we can rent this idea, if we can't afford to buy it?"
6. "If we can't handle it today, can we take an option out on it, giving us the time to get organized and do some market research before we invest?"
7. "Will it really turn people on?" It will if it earns superlatives when people talk about it. It will if it's truly beautiful. It will if it inspires and uplifts people.

Yes, a positive mental attitude toward ideas is basic to the skeletal structure of a successful Possibility Thinker!

VIII
Are You Ready to Choose a Positive Mental Attitude Toward DECISION MAKING?

Many of the positive mental attitudes can be wiped out by a decision to think negatively instead of positively. So the positive mental attitude toward decision making is fundamental and basic.

A. *The Possibility Thinker recognizes that every decision involves some risk.* There is no such thing as a totally safe decision. Show me an illustration of a so-called totally safe decision, and I will tell you it is a foregone conclusion, which means it's not a decision! A decision means there's a choice between alternatives and options, which may require choosing the good against the bad. But more often than not the risk may be of choosing the lesser good, which competes with the better good. As a pastor I've often had to tell people that most of our sins are the result not of blatant evil tempting us as much as of the downward pull of the lesser good, which distracts us from the greater good that merits our whole-hearted commitment!

B. *The Possibility Thinker knows that even indecision is a decision.* Sometimes going slowly is wise. On the other hand, it may turn out to be a pitiful and costly procrastination. Doing nothing doesn't mean you haven't made a decision. If laziness, indifference, or apathy result, you've made a decision to surrender leadership of your life rather than maintain control of your thoughts and feelings. Not to set goals and not to control your thinking are themselves decisions to be irresponsible! For our level of responsibility is measured by our ability to confront the decision-making process without unnecessary delay or distraction.

A positive mental attitude on decision making creates a Possibility Thinker who (1) is not afraid of taking risks and (2) who analyzes all possible risks carefully and bravely without self-deception! You're not being an impossibility thinker when you ask people to show you what's wrong with an idea or tell you the downside possibilities or tell you the worst thing that could happen. Persons with positive mental attitudes toward decision making don't want surprises. We want to anticipate every negative potential so that we can take out insurance, establish protective buffer zones, invent visible or invisible shields, or provide a parachute in case a bailout is necessary. Our positive attitude toward risk provides us with a positive mental attitude toward potential damage control in case the project takes a mortal blow. We believe in good luck, but we would rather be prepared!

Preparation and follow-through become the natural qualities that stand out about Possibility Thinkers who have a positive mental attitude toward decision making. We test ideas. The last thing we do is discard an idea that holds some positive potential in it. We understand that every good idea has something wrong with it. Every positive proposal has within itself some negative aspects. But we assume that the decision-making process can allow us either to eliminate the negative element or insulate the negative impact of the negative element in the idea and then to go on and exploit the positive.

So we focus on research and development.

We take a good look at risk reduction and risk control.

We focus on preparation, acquiring all of the information possible.

We believe in checking, double-checking, rechecking.

We consider the timing, which can be crucial.

We take a good look at communications. Who is going to tell whom about this decision?

Most importantly, we make certain that our decisions are based upon problems that beg for solutions and not upon our own ego needs.

No wonder Possibility Thinkers make great decisions more often than not! We are smart. We are good. We are tough! We are a success.

Applaud yourself! For you are on the way to becoming a great human being! You are changing from an impossibility thinker to a Possibility Thinker. That's marvelous, miraculous personality restructuring for success!

When You're Thru Changing . . .

. . . You're Thru!

CHAPTER 6

Packing the Power of Possibility Thinking into Your Life!

*R*eady? Let's put Possibility Thinking into practice. Let's have the fun of watching an impossibility thinker turn into a Possibility Thinker.

If you have accepted the basic positive mental attitudes, then I'm ready to turn you into a dynamic, success-oriented Possibility Thinker! Remember, Possibility Thinking, like success, is a process. So let's get on with learning how to practice, exercise, and apply Possibility Thinking to our mental activity. Let's get down to the business of turning your life around:

From dreaming to doing.

From negative thinking to positive thinking.

From failure to success.

From success to ongoing and growing success.

An ancient legend tells the story of a wise old hermit who lived in a log cabin high in the mountains. He was reputed to know the answer to any question ever brought to him. Well, one day two mischievous boys decided they were going to play a trick on the old fellow. They would ask him a question he couldn't answer!

After plotting one night, high in the loft of a dark barn, they shot a blinding light into a sparrow's eyes. Quickly they picked the stunned bird up and made their way to the old man's cabin. One of them could feel the bird's frightened, fluttering heartbeat in his hand as he held it snugly. Now, with their hands behind their backs they would pull a trick on the old man. They'd say, "What do we have in our hands?" And if he guessed a bird, they'd say, "What kind of a bird?" If he guessed the sparrow, then they would trap him! They would ask the trick question: "Tell us, wise one, is it dead or alive?" If he said "alive," they would squeeze the life out of the sparrow and prove him wrong. If he said, "It's dead," they'd prove him wrong again by simply letting the little creature fly!

They walked up the mountain trail, flashed the light on the log cabin, and knocked on the door. They waited nervously, their shaky hands behind them. The heavy door squeaked slowly open. There stood a huge old man with long hair and a white beard hanging almost to his waist. He glowered at them through his narrow eyes and said, "What is it, my boys?"

Excited, they answered, "Sir, wise old man, tell us if you can, what do we hold in our hands?"

His eyes pierced through them. He waited. Then he spoke. "A bird."

They said, "Well, Sir, what kind of a bird?"

"A sparrow."

They poked each other. "Tell us, old man, is it dead or alive?"

He looked and looked and thought. And finally he spoke, "As you will have it, my boys!"

What do you hold in your hand right now? Your destiny! Your future! Is it dead or alive? Your dreams! Are they dead or alive? The answer is: As you will have it, my friends!

Enough philosophizing. Let's get to work and remodel your mental processes, retuning and retooling your thinking to succeed! Follow me carefully. I know the path well. I've walked it many times. I've been a guide to thousands. Just trust me. I really care about you!

Sterilize Your *ATTITUDE!*

In the last chapter we reviewed the positive mental attitudes that form the foundation of Possibility Thinking. Don't kid yourself. Residual negatives always linger or easily, naturally, and swiftly return to do their damage. Remember: Problems aren't meant to stop you. They're meant to be solved! Right now let's solve the first and ever-recurring problem, the tendency to drop back into old patterns of negative thinking.

It's shocking how seductively, secretly, and furtively negative thoughts infiltrate the intimate and innocent living quarters of our minds where they assault, violate, and defile our youthful dreams.

Have you ever seen people walking the beach with a metal detector? Metal detectors can find money, watches, jewelry, and even scraps of junk hidden in the sand. They provide an interesting hobby and help keep the beaches clear of rubbish.

Recall, now, those open door frames for the security check at airline terminals. Green light! Walk through! Uh-oh! Red lights flash. Buzzers go off. "Walk through again, Sir," the security agent orders. You comply, only to set off the alarm again. "Empty your pockets, Sir."

"Oh, yes, my nail clipper!"

We all need a similar detector in our lives, but rather than a metal detector, we need a MENTAL detector to detect both positive attitudes and negative attitudes so that we can keep our MENTAL state as clear of negativity as possible.

Let me alert you to what will set off the "Negative Thinking Alarm Bell."

First there are the negative assumptions we all carry with us. Undetected and unexposed, these silent assumptions will do damage.

Illustration: "I don't believe in religion."

Translation: The silent assumption is that if you become

a vital Christian you'll have to be a "Holy Joe"—a pious, perfect, joyless, boring person. Wrong! A pitifully erroneous assumption!

Illustration: "I have to be rich or well connected socially to get started."

Translation: The silent assumption is that because you're from a poor family with severe limitations you must not dream of success! Wrong! Wrong! Wrong!

Illustration: "I know what I'm doing. I've got it made! I'll do it my way."

Translation: The silent assumption is that all of your answers are right! And no one is smarter or wiser than you. And you can dream dreams, set goals, plunge ahead, without getting the best advice possible! That's sad!

Not surprisingly, a few of the silent assumptions that block or sink us result from negative programming. For instance, we are slow to question what we have been taught in our universities. We assume all of our teachers were always right! But over and over again the experts have come up with new findings. What we believed to be *absolute* has turned out to be *obsolete*! But we still allow those presumed absolutes to limit our thinking and hinder our progress.

Another alarm bell on our MENTAL detector should sound when we hear ourselves saying, "I've never done this before!" Don't let inexperience become an excuse for not trying! Don't let it intimidate you! Possibility Thinkers break through the barrier of inexperience by simply starting. Rembrandt was a beginner once! Einstein started in basic math. Every superstar in the big leagues began as a rookie.

Think of the colossal waste of human potential, energy, growth, and creativity that occurs when we allow inexperience to hold us back. To break through, you must adopt the attitude that inexperience will not defeat you. Never give in to the attitude that you lack experience to make your dream come true, for courage and a positive attitude are far more important.

I am reminded of the story of the little boy overheard talking to himself as he strutted through the backyard, baseball cap in place, toting ball and bat. "I'm the greatest baseball player in the world," he said proudly. Then he tossed the ball into the air, swung at it, and missed. Undaunted, he picked up the ball, threw it into the air and said again, "I'm the greatest ball player ever!" He swung at the ball. And again he missed.

He paused a moment to carefully examine his bat and ball. Then once again he threw the ball into the air. "I'm the greatest baseball player who ever lived!" he said. He swung the bat hard and again missed the ball. "Strike three!" he shouted, adding, "Wow! What a pitcher!"

There's nothing like a positive mental attitude! It can give us the courage to attempt anything! Do you lack experience? That's wonderful! You have a new and fresh adventure ahead of you!

> "Grieve not for me who am about to start
> A new adventure.
> Eager I stand and ready to depart,
> Me and my reckless, pioneering heart."[1]

Sterilize your attitude the way a doctor makes sure he is protected from passing on, or catching, infections. Challenge the negative attitudes that may actually be distortions rising from negative assumptions: distortions like "The law will never allow it" (based on the assumption that the law can't be changed); distortions like "We can't afford it" (based on the assumption that the money cannot be saved, earned, borrowed, or acquired through the sale of assets).

Challenge every single impossibility idea or negative attitude that still lurks furtively in the back of your mind. Dig out, unveil, expose, uncover, unmask every one of them! Examine until you uncover silent assumptions that lead to distorted thinking! Clear out every one of them! Bias? Ignorance? Blind spot? Distortion? Clean them out! Clear them up!

Mind you, it's a constant discipline that must be set up in the process of successful thinking!

---

[1]Anonymous.

Analyze Your *POSSIBILITIES!*

If you have sterilized your attitude of the mental bacteria of negative thinking, your mind now welcomes what otherwise would have been perceived as ridiculous, impossible suggestions. Now they appear as possibilities, opportunities!

Let's go! Throw wide open the windows of your imagination and let the incredible possibilities come in! What dreams would you dream if you knew you could succeed?

Would you become a doctor—when you're past fifty years of age? Cory SerVaas did! You can read her column in every issue of *The Saturday Evening Post*!

My own daughter, Carol, after they amputated her left leg, dreamed of becoming a competitive skier. She went on to win gold medals!

I'll never forget a book autograph party in Brooklyn. Hundreds were waiting in line to have me sign a book they had purchased. The first person in line was a handsome, well-dressed, obviously successful man. "Dr. Schuller, I'm twenty-eight years old. I started watching you fourteen years ago in my family's crowded and poor apartment. You told me I could accomplish anything if I was a Possibility Thinker!

"I got your books. I became a Christian! I thought, 'If I knew I would not fail, I'd become a lawyer!' You said I was free to choose any dream . . . free to set any goal! I was free to succeed if I was willing to pay the price!

"Well, Dr. Schuller, I'm now a member of the bar in the State of New York! And my goal is to be licensed to practice before the Supreme Court! I know I'll make it! I don't need your autograph! I've been standing in line here for two hours for something I *do* need, and that is to thank you for making me a Possibility Thinker!"

Recognize Your *POSITION!*

It must be said at this point that Possibility Thinkers don't go off with wild and wacky moves, ignoring reality. Before you plunge into a possibility, recognize your position.

Don't Try to Launch a Missile from a Canoe!

Become aware of what might be called the "positioning principle" in marketing. No matter what possibilities you're latching onto, no matter what dreams you may be pursuing, you'll have to be a successful salesman. Somehow your product or service has to be marketed to make sure that people who would benefit from your creativity know that your contribution is now available to them.

The wise Possibility Thinker will take stock of what position can be found in the marketplace. He'll begin by reviewing any competition. Then he'll re-examine unfulfilled human need. Is there an open niche that no one else is filling?

A top corporate executive at Ford Motor Company once told me, "We've been frustrated trying to strengthen our position in the luxury car market. We haven't succeeded in dislodging Mercedes. They've got their position set so strongly. It's rough."

One of the reasons our ministry succeeded was that our church offered positive-thinking Christianity without dogmatism. We have succeeded in national religious television because our position in the marketplace of religious ideas is clearly defined. And we have little competition. In the United States of America there are millions of people who want a positive, practical, intelligent, classical presentation of Christianity. We provide that on the "Hour of Power" to the best of our abilities.

To storm full-speed ahead because of your ego needs or your own enthusiasm and disregard competition or the harsh realities of the positioning principle in marketing could prove disastrous. We have to be prepared to alter our course according to the unsatisfied wants of human beings.

The story is told of Her Royal Majesty's private yacht cruising through the summer seas with Prince Charles and Princess Di on board. After a delightful dinner with the royal couple, the captain asked to be excused to return to the bridge and "check on our progress."

As soon as he stepped to the bridge, he clearly saw lights approaching him on a collision course. He barked a command to the signal master, "Tell them to alter their course."

The signal went out. "Alter your course."

Immediately the approaching lights returned the message, "You alter your course."

The captain was affronted. "We signaled first. You alter your course," was his next message.

Immediately the stranger's lights signaled, "Cannot comply. You must alter your course."

The indignant captain ordered the signal master, "Tell them who we are and who we have on board!"

The signal master sent out the message, "This is Captain John Smith. This is Her Royal Majesty's private yacht. We have on board Prince Charles and Princess Diana. This is a royal directive: *You will alter your course!*"

For a brief second there was nothing but darkness in the distance. Then the lights reappeared with this signal: "This is Fred Smith. I've been in charge of this lighthouse for twenty years!"

Even if someone already has your position in the marketplace wrapped up, don't immediately discard your dream. You might be able to get a percentage or win over a part of the competitor's following. But before you do, ask yourself, "Will I be satisfied with a small percentage of the market at the outset?" Many small businesses are succeeding today because their overhead and income expectations are considerably lower than the competition's. Still others are succeeding because the competition offers poor service.

But many businesses are successful because they are first in their position with the most. Racers know the advantage of a good "pole" position. The person who is first with the best is in an enviable position for sure! Perhaps that's a possibility for you! It just might be if you change your position by altering your course, one way or another.

Scrutinize Your VALUES!

Now you are ready for this most important step in the process of success: Hold onto your values! Possibility Thinking without the restraints of wholesome values could lead you to hell! For instance: Do you want to become superrich? Well, without the values of the time-tested Ten Commandments, without a respect for law and order, you could turn into a criminal! Success at any price is hellish folly! "For what will it profit you," Jesus Christ asked, "if you gain the whole world, and lose your own soul?" (Mark 8:36).

So you have dreams! Great! Check them by the highest value system. I know of no textbook on ethics or human values that surpasses the Bible. Get one. Read it. Test your possibilities in the light of this classic textbook!

"I wanted to be a star in Hollywood so badly I set aside the moral teachings I learned in Sunday school. I slept with my agent. He promised he'd get me good parts. I got them! And herpes simplex too!" The actress wept while sharing her story with me. She repented! I cried!

Speaking before the American Bankers Association in San Francisco, I challenged them to ask themselves three questions: (1) What are we in this business for anyway? (2) If we keep going at it the way we are, will we get what we're going after? (3) If we succeed in reaching our goals, will we be satisfied—and proud of how we did it? I wrapped up my speech by saying, "Remember that at the bottom line of your business of banking, there are no numbers! Only people!"

To keep your values on target, remember so to live that when you "arrive," you'll have pride behind you, love around you, and hope ahead of you. Then success is truly the path to heaven.

Dr. Charles S. Judd, Jr., died in Honolulu as I was writing this chapter. Bob Krauss, columnist in the *Honolulu Advertiser*, wrote:

> *A rainbow appeared in the sky over Central Union Church, a fitting benediction to Dr. Judd's memorial service. Who was Dr. Charles Sheldon Judd, Jr.? His wife, Mary, often called him "Dr. No Charge." She worked in the office and collected the fees.*
>
> *"When a patient couldn't afford to pay, Charlie wrote 'No charge' on a slip of paper," she said. "I used to have a box full of them."*
>
> *. . . There hasn't been a bigger outpouring of aloha at a funeral in Honolulu as long as I can re-*

member. The whole church yard was filled with cars. Inside, people stood against the walls and in doorways. . . .

The most impressive tribute came from the people of Western Samoa. They presented Mary, in the name of their chief of state, Tanu Masili Malietoa, a fine mat and a tapa.

Samoans often present mats and tapas.

But the Rev. Sualauvi Tuimalealiifono explained that this presentation, coming from the highest level, was special. "The presentation is reserved for Samoan chiefs and royalty," he said.

It has been made only once before to a foreigner. That was in the last century to Robert Louis Stevenson. "This is the first time it has been made outside of Western Samoa," Tuimalealiifono said.

The Samoans were expressing their gratitude for the work Charlie did there as a government doctor from 1965 to 1969.

Mary and Charlie worked until he had seen every patient waiting on the lawn. Many had come by jitney bus from the other end of the island.

They called him "Savior." People stopped him on the main street of Apia to show him the scars of the operations he had performed.

Speakers at the memorial service talked about Charlie's gentleness. And he was as close to a saint as any man I've known. But Father Damien and St. Francis of Assisi didn't achieve what they did only by being gentle.

Charlie, like them, was strong. He had a will! On an average day at the free medical clinic in Kalihi, he'd see twenty-seven patients in two hours after being up half the night on an emergency.

It was an amazing combination of gentleness and strength. I think that's why the rainbow appeared over Central Union Church after the service.[2]

---

[2]*Honolulu Advertiser.*

Itemize Your *ASSETS!*

If your hopes appear fantastic and your dreams only un-realistic impossibilities, hang in there! Now's the time to check, double-check, and recheck your assets. What do you have going for you? The freedom to try? If you live in America, chances are you do! Don't forget—the lack of freedom is the really big obstacle to success, and that problem has already been solved! You're free to study, to strive, to work, to save, to start succeeding at any enterprise or endeavor you have chosen! Ask yourself this question: "What am I doing with the freedom I have?"

Move on. Move ahead. Make a complete list of your financial assets. You aren't as poor as you may think! Yes, there are the obvious assets—cash, real estate, clothes, jewelry. But there are also hidden assets—knowledge, experience, freedom, friends, faith.

Don't forget your hidden, undeveloped potential! "I never knew you had it in you!" a mother said to her successful son.

"Neither did I, Mom! It's like coming into an inheritance I never expected!"

Every person has forgotten or undiscovered assets. We all have potential for greatness. The problem is recognizing, discovering, tapping, and developing them to their fullest.

My grandson, Jason, age four, complained one day, "I don't know what I want to be when I grow up. I can't be a policeman because I don't have fast enough shoes to catch the criminals. I can't be a fireman because I'll get burned up. I can't be an ambulance driver because I'm not strong enough to pick up the bed."

His mother, replied, "Well, Jason, maybe you could be a preacher like Grandpa."

"Oh no! I couldn't do that!"

"Why not?"

"I wouldn't know what to say!"

The young aren't the only ones who have difficulty in recognizing their assets. I remember visiting a church when I was a student in seminary. I met a lady there and asked her, "What do you do in the church?"

"Oh," she said, "I don't have any talent."

I said, "What do you mean?"

"Well, I can't sing. And I—I get tongue-tied, so I can't teach. I just don't have any talents, but people kept saying, 'You've got such a pretty smile.' I know it's very important for the church to be a friendly place, so I decided to stand at the door and that's what I do. I'm not an usher and I'm not a greeter, but I just stand there and smile them in and I smile them out."

That was her gift. "Do not neglect the gift that is in you" (1 Tim. 4:14). Everybody has a talent, a divine gift.

Venita Van Caspel is the number one certified financial planner in America today. Many of her books have made the *New York Times* best-seller list.

Venita is someone who learned how to itemize and develop assets. She was raised in a loving Christian home with no money, which she claims gave her a very healthy respect for a dollar. So she decided that if she ever got one, she'd better learn what to do with it. She worked her way through college while studying economics and finance. While she was in college, she married and put her knowledge on the shelf for a number of years.

Then her husband was killed in a plane accident. She received a small insurance settlement and decided that she had better do the very best she could with it. She could not afford to make a mistake! So she went back to college and studied investments, learned what to do with her own money, and became very interested in helping other people with theirs.

While she was in school, she heard a very startling statistic. Of every one hundred people reaching age sixty-five, only 2 percent were financially independent. She felt that this was a tragedy, and so she decided that she would help people become financially independent. That became her mission, her Christian vocation, for she wanted to make the best use of her God-given talents.

Venita went on to become the first woman to own a seat on the Pacific Coast Stock Exchange. Many of the most important people in the country are her clients, seeking her guidance daily. She turned her education, which had been a dead asset, into a live asset—a profitable, rewarding profession.

We all have dead assets that can be turned into live assets. Someone has a paint brush and oils which they haven't picked up for a long time. Somebody else owns a violin that has been in the case for years. And someone else has not sat down at a piano or opened a music book. Are you a writer? When was the last time you went to that typewriter?

Itemize your assets! Don't become negative about yourself when people haven't given you adequate recognition—even if you were told that you weren't particularly talented or intelligent, even if you were told once that your painting wasn't very good, your music was poor, or your dancing mediocre.

Do you know that over the fireplace mantel of the late Fred Astaire's house in Beverly Hills hung an enlightening memo? It was written by the casting director of the show that was being produced when Fred Astaire first auditioned. The memo says:

> "Name: Fred Astaire
> Comments: Can't act, slightly bald, can dance a
> little."

Itemize your assets—review them carefully. You may be stronger, richer, better positioned to move ahead with your possibilities than you ever imagined!

Capitalize On Your EXPERIENCES!

We all know that capital is anything we can invest to expand our productivity. And coming up with the capital is one of the first major hurdles in starting a new venture.

The good news for you is that you can even turn your failures into an investment that can increase your productivity! It's true! Have you failed? Many people will want to know why. Capitalize on their curiosity! You can become a consultant!

When I was called to start a new church in Southern California thirty-seven years ago, I first had to itemize my assets. My assets at that time amounted to myself, my wife, Arvella, who could play the organ, and five hundred dollars in cash. That was the sum of my capital.

Somehow, I had to think of a creative way to turn those assets into a church. The first step was finding a place to hold the service. The Seventh Day Adventist Church, the Elks Club, and the funeral home were all taken. I felt as though I had failed even before I started!

But then one day while looking at the newspaper, I happened to see the movie section. It advertised a movie that was going to be showing at the new drive-in theatre. Suddenly, I got the idea. I went to see the manager of the drive-in theatre. He agreed that I could use it for church services. But I was the butt of many jokes. The truth is I had failed at all other possibilities and was now at the bottom—church in a drive-in theatre. But I fell in love with the idea of being able to worship under the sky, the sun, and the clouds! Twenty years later that idea would inspire an all-glass church where I could see the sky again! The Crystal Cathedral was the result of my failure to find a "hall" to start a church!

So, if you have failed, don't dismay. It could be the very best thing that ever happened to you. Because of your loss you may now be free to make a change that you should have made a long time ago, but never would have had the courage to attempt.

I cannot tell you how many men and women have come to me over the years and said, "When I lost my job, I thought the world had come to an end. But then something even greater came along." One person started her own business; another was free to accept a new job opportunity that afforded more freedom, more creativity, and better pay.

Prioritize Your *GOALS!*

Surely, success does not happen until you set a goal. And every time you set a new goal you have to rearrange your priorities. That's not easy. It can be rough. But remember your biggest problem is inside your own head. Maybe you will have to give up a pet project for a while. You might have to forego some of your other goals in order to make this new move. This might be the year when you will have to reassign projects to others or to a back burner in order to exploit the opportunity that won't wait. I've had to do this many times during the thirty-plus years I've been in ministry.

List all of your (a) obligations, (b) hobbies, (c) outside commitments, (d) attractive ideas. Now be prepared to weigh carefully the value of the demands made upon you. Have the strength to make the right move. Remember: *It takes guts to leave the ruts.* Carefully check the impossibility thoughts that may enter your mind to torpedo your important dream.

You might be able to hire people to do a lot of the work that you're doing today. I have been able to develop a church, write books, and carry out a television ministry because *I don't do anything if I can possibly hire somebody else to do it. That leaves me with a few things that I am convinced I and I alone can and must do. Within that frame of reference I'm ready to set my priorities.* On Sundays it probably means I'm preaching at the pulpit of the Crystal Cathedral. On Monday nights it means that I'm on a private date with my wife. During the summer season, I'm traveling abroad in ministry and study, or I'm in isolation writing my books.

Get your priorities straight, and you'll be geared up for success.

Reorganize Your *CALENDAR!*

Now mark your calendar. It is incredibly simple and easy to maintain control over your goals if you will only learn to write them down on the calendar. Once you've rearranged your priorities, you'll have to reorganize your calendar! Perhaps you have determined that this is the time for fence-mending with family, friends, or business associates. If that's the case, you have to take time to be sociable. Mark some dates on the calendar to give yourself affectionately and wholeheartedly to those whom you have perhaps neglected.

The top priority now is to think through your next move and to do some long-range planning. Mark your calendar for "think time." I know one very successful person who schedules sixty minutes every day for thinking time! With him this includes prayer, Bible reading, and private meditation. But during this hour he is isolated and protected from uninvited, unwelcome, pressure-producing interruptions. Only for urgent messages from his immediate family will his secretary dare to interrupt this important activity.

Perhaps the next priority for you is to do research and testing to determine whether your next project is feasible. So you will reorganize your calendar to make time for meetings with informed consultants.

Have you noticed you've been changing the last year or two? Have you noticed new frictions, frustrations, or fatigue that you haven't noticed before? You'll probably need to reorganize your calendar to allow for times of fun and rest. My goals have always been to maximize my personal and professional success but at the same time maintain health of mind and body and harmony in my marriage and family. For that reason I periodically have a "calendar meeting" with my wife and top staff. We block out—a year in advance—rest time, study time, and travel time.

Just be aware of this: Control your calendar for your calendar will control you!

Visualize Your OBJECTIVES!

You are ready now to start drawing pictures or writing down your "will-do" list. (Be sure to put dates on your calendar!) The mind is an amazing, mysterious, marvelous instrument. There was a revealing article in the May 1985 issue of *Psychology Today* entitled "In the Mind's Eye." I recommend it for further study. Basically, the article deals with the process of visualization. The visualization is not physical vision but inner vision. It uses the power of imagination. The Bible also talks about a similar concept: "Where there is no vision, the people perish" (Prov. 29:18).

I have found that once my dreams were turned into pictures, I took a giant step toward achieving my goals. In one instance I started by retaining an architect. We talked through the project. We analyzed whether or not it would meet authentic need. Finally, the artist produced a water color rendering. At that point my goal took on the appearance of reality. I photographed it in my mind, filed it in my memory. It became a motivating part of my subconscious. I find that I have to be able to visualize or envision an objective before I connect to an energy source that will give me the drive to pursue the project through the challenging phases ahead.

In visualizing your objectives, focusing becomes extremely important. Dr. David Burns, author of *Feeling Good: The New Mood Therapy,* is one of the leading practitioners of a psychological therapy called cognitive therapy. He uses the illustration of binoculars. "If you don't have a vision for your life," he points out, "then you haven't probably focused in on anything."[3]

Take out your mental binoculars and focus on the specific objective you wish to accomplish. With your imagination as your direction finder, aim your attention until it is pointed specifically at a measurable and manageable objective. See it. Seize it emotionally, and it will seize you!

While you are focusing on your inner vision and your heart's desire, use a filter. There may be many confusing images in your mind. Any ambiguities of internal vision can cause competition for your intense enthusiasm and defuse

---

[3]David Burns, *Feeling Good: The New Mood Therapy* (New York: William Morrow, 1980).

your drive and power to move forcefully ahead. For many persons this is their constant problem. They are like travelers on a tour bus, looking out of the window, watching all of the sights passing by, but never really seeing or feeling any one of the places that pass too swiftly in front of their eyes.

Interestingly enough I have learned a great deal of psychology and theology from my years of close association with great architects. When it came time to build our first walk-in, drive-in sanctuary (which we eventually outgrew), I contacted one of the great architects of the twentieth century, the late Richard Neutra. When we discussed the design he would say to me, "Bob, we've got to build buildings that will help you in your work. Before we draw any pictures or create any sketches, we have to get back to the basics. You will want a building that will make it easy for positive emotions to flow into people and a building that will, hopefully, block out negative thoughts."

Needless to say I was intrigued. The truth is I had already visualized the kind of church building I wanted. What's very important and interesting is that in this stage of Possibility Thinking—visualizing the objective—we can still make adaptations that affect the ultimate success or failure of the project.

"What do you mean, Mr. Neutra?" I asked.

"Well, we simply look at symbols that produce negativity in the subconscious mind. Then we design a structure that will block out negative impulses from the brain and focus on the positive emotional sources and centers."

He could tell that I wasn't with him and didn't understand. He made it simple.

"For instance," and with his slender hand, he pointed a bony finger at a power pole, "over there's a power pole. When the subconscious receives the image of the power pole, tension is produced within the personality. The subconscious knows that if you touched those hot wires you would be electrocuted. So wherever there is a material object that would produce a negative emotion, we'll simply build a solid wall so you won't see it! On the other hand, where there is a beautiful view which would bring tranquility into the mind, that's where we'll put solid glass windows to focus on the positive! We would never build a solid wall that would block out the possibility of a positive emotion entering through the scenery of sky, ocean, or gardens. The pictures we sketch will be determined by the input we want to invite into our personalities."

Well, you can be certain that Mr. Neutra's concept drastically changed my visions of what a church building should be like! Previously I had seen a conventional structure with a solid ceiling, windows lined up like soldiers in formation on either side, and a solid wall behind the pulpit. After visualizing our objectives we clarified our concepts and made some important corrections that so sold us on our own visions that unbelievable energy was released. No wonder we did not fail!

Frequently people tell me that they have a dream and want to come in and talk about it. I usually give them the same reply: "I don't think I have the time to listen until you've taken the time to think it through." I then offer this advice: "Draw me a picture. Put it in words, if you are not an artist. Try to condense your project into a single page. Unless and until you're able to clarify it, you're probably not ready to move ahead."

So you've got the picture? The vision is clear? Negative thoughts and errors that could defeat it have been filtered out? You're focused sharply on what you want to accomplish? Good! Then we can move ahead.

But wait a minute. Are you sure your vision is the right size? You see it, but have you sized it correctly? Only through careful prayer can you determine whether the dimension of your dream is in proper proportion to your person and your position. Some people bite off too big a chunk, and they choke on it. Start small! Achieve a little success. Establish a solid base. And then branch out.

On the other hand, some people think too small. If you can achieve the dream without the help of God, then it is too small. Make your dreams big enough for God to fit in, for God's dreams are always so large that they require His help to make them come true. This is God's built-in defense system to keep us humble. Then when the success is realized, we'll not forget who really gets the credit!

If you have seen your project clearly and have sized it correctly, then seize it! Make your goal firm, and seal it with an inner intention. Determine that you're going to make it happen. Even if it appears impossible, move ahead. Do you want your dream to succeed? See it! Size it! Seize it! Feel it! And succeed!

Mobilize Your *RESOURCES!*

Now is the time to give it all you've got! Most persons fail, not because they lack talent, training, opportunity, but because the project doesn't get their or their leader's whole-hearted attention. As a practitioner of Possibility Thinking, I've been wholeheartedly and passionately committed to each project I've undertaken. Each time I've seen clearly in my mind what the finished project could be like: a building; a book; a television program; a family; a house. Then I was prepared to put everything on the line to accomplish my objective. The resources were pooled to keep everything concentrated on reaching the immediate goal.

This is the time for a total, all-out effort. It's America's response after Pearl Harbor. It's the invasion of Normandy. Centralize power. Mobilize resources. This is the time to cut down on sleep and work longer hours. Reserve no energy. Mortgage everything, if needed, to get this thing off the ground. Gain a firm foothold. Stubbornly hold the initial gains. Be like an "iron peg hammered in frozen ground, immovable"—to use Winston Churchill's words concerning one of his greater generals!

Pour your most passionate prayers into this project. Call upon the wisest and the bravest minds you know about. Call a famous leader in the field, and sell him on going to work for you on this exciting project! You may need to check your connection to that ultimate power source, Jesus Christ. "I can do all things through Christ who strengthens me."

Surely you'll need all of the spiritual, financial, intellectual, and professional resources possible—and all of the energy possible! Super achievers, champions, top producers have to have the physical energy to work long hours and at a fast pace.

Energize Your *THINKING!*

Once you have 1) sterilized your attitudes, 2) analyzed the possibilities, 3) recognized your position, 4) scrutinized your values, 5) itemized your assets, 6) capitalized on your experiences, 7) prioritized your goals, 8) reorganized your calendar, 9) visualized your objectives, and 10) mobilized your resources, then you are ready to 11) energize your thinking with a massive injection of enthusiasm. Enthusiasm *is* energy!

What is enthusiasm? It is that mysterious something that turns an average person into an outstanding individual. It makes an old person young, and without it a young person becomes old. It is the hidden spring of endless energy. It is that beautiful force that carries us from mediocrity to excellence. It turns on a bright light in a dull face until the eyes sparkle and the personality brightens with joy. It is the spiritual magnet that attracts helpful and happy people to become our fruitful friends. It is the joyful emotional fountain that bubbles up, attracting persons to come to our side and drink from the joy that rises out of our heart. It is the happy song of a positive person who sings an inspiring message to the world: "I can! It's possible! We'll do it."

Enthusiasm is that long-sought-after fountain of eternal life. Old men stop to drink of its elixir and suddenly dream new dreams. Marvelous, miraculous, mysterious new strength surges through the old bones. Discouragement fades like the morning fog in the shining sun. Suddenly you catch yourself whistling, noticing birds flying, seeing the glorious shape of the white clouds against blue sky. From deep within yourself a new song breaks forth. You whistle. You sing. Now you are alive again!

Enthusiasm—what is it? How do you explain this mountain-melting power? How can you get it? The word comes from two Greek words, *"en"* and *"Theos."* Literally translated they mean "in-God." We speak of such persons as inspired. IN-SPIRITED people! Fill your life with the God Spirit and all kinds of power break forth.

No one will get anywhere in life if they lack energetic thinking. Now use a pen and paper in your enthusiastic exercise of Possibility Thinking. Enthusiastically write down your energetic thoughts and list all the goals you want to accomplish.

Every housewife knows how important a written list can be. Have you ever noticed how many young homemakers push their carts through the grocery aisles while referring to their grocery lists? Those simple grocery lists are the secret to saving time and money, and to avoiding frustration. Aisle after aisle of tempting packages has been designed to catch their eyes and divert their attention, but written lists keep them focused on grocery needs and away from things like a box of gooey fudge cookies.

I love the story of the elderly couple who one evening wanted some ice cream. The lady said to her husband, "Why don't you go out and get us some ice cream?"

When he agreed to go, she said, "Make sure it's vanilla, not chocolate, and write it down or you'll forget it."

"I won't forget," he protested.

As he was going out the door, she said, "Don't *forget* the chocolate sauce. Not strawberry topping, but chocolate."

"No problem—I won't forget!"

As he was getting in the car, she opened the window and called out, "And get some nuts too!"

"Yes, dear." He drove off. His intentions were the best, but when he got to the store he couldn't remember what it was he was supposed to get. He walked up and down the aisles trying to remember.

When he got home, his wife was horrified at what he had purchased. All he had was a dozen eggs.

She said, "What? A dozen eggs? I knew you'd forget! You forgot the bacon!"

We all need lists! When we have no projects, no causes, no issues, no concerns, no dreams, we become listless, which is just one stage above depression. We need an "I-would-like-to-do" list. We need an "I-wish-I-could-do" list. We need a "Wouldn't-it-be-fantastic?" list. Look at your list of possibilities every day, and every day you'll be enthused.

If you're listless—it could be because you're list-less!

At a seminar I attended some time ago I heard someone ask a doctor, "Why is it that some people have more energy than others?"

He replied, "It's largely a matter of glands. Some people have energetic genes." He went on to point out that the endocrine glands are mostly responsible for rushing the adrenalin into the blood.

But I wasn't satisfied. I asked, "What causes the glands to activate the adrenalin?"

The doctor answered, "The difference is that some people's glands get stimulated and put out energy, while others don't get stimulated and don't put out energy."

I asked, "What is the stimulation that causes the gland to secrete energy-producing chemicals?"

His answer was, "Possibility Thinking. You know that, Dr. Schuller!"

Negative emotions such as doubt, fear, worry, anger, hostility, self-pity, and jealousy will drain you of your energy. Likewise, indecision saps energy. Commitment, on the other hand, taps into and releases incredible powers—physical, emotional, and spiritual. If you've got the faith, God's got the power. He wants to open floodgates of energy in the person who experiences his faith and gets going. As you spend yourself building, constructing, helping, and pursuing great causes, you become tremendously enthusiastic. You don't consume energy; you recycle your energy supply!

So, dare to dream, catch a vision, make a list of things you could do to help others who are hurting. In a world where so many people are beset by pain and hurt, we could write many lists. With all the emotional and physical pain, hunger, starvation, and strife, there's no excuse for not catching an enthusiastic vision of what you can do and be!

Organize Your *NETWORK!*

A careful analysis of every successful individual and institution will reveal an obvious or obscure network that makes for success. Consider the network of blood vessels that pervades our bodies—from massive arteries entering the heart to miniature capillaries that feed every living cell. There's no way that one, big, powerful heart could succeed without the network! In the same way a network of nerves fans and filters out from the brain to every single tissue to send and deliver messages. And there's no way the mighty mind could succeed in maintaining management control without this incredible network.

Our television ministry is aired over nearly two hundred television stations to nearly 90 percent of the people who live in the United States. We call these two hundred television stations our network.

Television air time is expensive. We have slowly, surely, solidly recruited and organized a network of twenty thousand donors who pledge five hundred to a thousand dollars a year to help pay for the air time. We call this our Eagles Club. It is our basic financial network without which we could not succeed.

Nearly two thousand volunteer members of our church have been recruited, trained, and organized to do the work of our local church ministry. They prepare Christmas boxes for the state prison; they maintain America's longest-running suicide prevention telephone ministry, twenty-four hours a day; they host and offer counseling to hundreds of thousands of visitors who come to our church campus each year. This is our network of workers without which we could never succeed!

What kind of a network of friends, coworkers, salesmen do you need? Think it through! Remember the positive mental attitude toward leadership. And remember the positive attitude toward people. Now build your organization on these solid foundations!

Start small. Test your systems and work the bugs out while you're small and have "hands-on" creative control. As it improves, expand your network. For it's time to get networking if you want to get success working.

Harmonize Your *CONFLICTS!*

Check out the really successful individuals and institutions and one thing stands out quickly and conspicuously. There's real harmony. Morale is high, releasing tremendous energy. That spells drive, productivity! Enthusiasm runs high. Production is at peak efficiency, with excellence of product and service. Sloppy workmanship, production delays, shoddy service are rarities.

You are ready now to see the urgency of this all-important exercise in practicing Possibility Thinking: Harmonize your conflicts.

Start by harmonizing your inner conflicts—the battles you fight within yourself when faced by a clash of values. You want to move ahead, yet you know it will hurt some people. By all means make sure you have a clear, dependable, unwavering set of moral and ethical principles—then go by the Book! And move ahead.

It's imperative that you harmonize your inner conflicts and deal with the inevitable contradictions. If not, you'll lack the enthusiasm and drive to succeed. A vacillating, wavering leadership will emerge, which spells "Failure waiting to happen." Positive prayer for divine guidance is absolutely essential! Be tough on yourself. You can't run with the hares and dash with the hounds.

Here moral fiber is woven into your leadership style. Say "yes" to what is right, "no" to what is wrong. And you'll find peace in your heart! Now you are strong enough to tackle the exterior conflicts!

Do not kid yourself; success without conflict is unrealistic. Every time you do anything noteworthy somebody will find fault. And, after all, you aren't perfect. No project is without its negative aspects. You can expect to generate a new set of tensions every time you set a new goal. And there's something wrong with every good idea. Be prepared for conflict.

Harmonize your conflicts early. Try to anticipate where and in whom you can expect conflict, disagreement, or disharmony to emerge. Before I make a forward move, I call together a collection of the wisest and most trusted advisors and teammates. Together we determine how we can prevent conflict! Conflict prevention is better than conflict resolution.

Neutralize Your *OPPOSITION!*

When conflict cannot be prevented, then resolution may be called for. To begin with try to turn enemies into friends. Treat the opposition with dignity. People who belittle people will be little people—and accomplish little!

For more years than I can recall I have conducted my board meetings with the let's-make-it-unanimous attitude. As the chairman of the board I would respect contrary opinions. I would seek to pry open the quiet person whose silence suggested private disagreement. "John," I would say respectfully, "I sense you have some reservations. Perhaps you're thinking of something we're overlooking?" Open discussion would move us toward a decision. "John, have we satisfied your concerns? And are you ready to vote with us on this? If not, let's wait, and between now and the next meeting, let's work out an agreeable compromise. We need everybody enthusiastically on board with this new project!"

Remember,

> The *demanding* person runs into resistance.
> The *defeated* person runs into indifference.
> The *dedicated* person runs into help![4]

By all means, give your opposition credit! They may be wrong, but even so, they're partly right. Listen and learn! Resolve the issues clearly and thoroughly in private rather than ignore the tension points and pay a price later in the marketplace.

---

[4]Schuller, *You Can Become*, 153.

Can all opposition be neutralized? Yes, most of the time. So try! But when the opposition is determined to deflate, defeat, and destroy your dream, then part ways. You may even need to initiate it. Deal with the conflict in a friendly, fair, frank, and firm manner. You'll sense a vast relief throughout the organization as the source of obstructionist forces is healthfully removed.

Minimize Your *RISKS!*

If you have resolved the inner and outer conflicts and handled the opposition constructively, you are still not home free. There may still be other risks to be considered. Become an expert in risk reduction, risk elimination, risk neutralization, and you're on your way toward being a top-ranking risk manager.

This will test and challenge your Possibility Thinking! Remember, you are a realist; there will always be the element of risk. But let the rewards of success, never the risk of failure, take the leadership post in your personal and professional life. Risks are challenges to meet—not excuses for backing out and quitting!

Nevertheless, I would never think of traveling by car, not even across my community, without a spare tire. I vote for parachutes. I opt for escape hatches. Every ship I've ever been on has had life jackets and lifeboats. Am I being negative? Not at all. I'm making sure that if the worst should happen I'll survive—to start over again! With this attitude I'm on the way toward making certain that if there's a failure, it will not be final!

When we envisioned the Crystal Cathedral it was projected to cost $10 million. Thirty percent inflation for three years running boosted that estimate by $3 million a year to a final cost of nearly $20 million! We were under construction without a complete financing package. Unless we raised cash, construction would be halted. Banks shied away from construction loans. Suddenly—my church board thought miraculously—a leading California bank offered a $10 million construction and "take out" (meaning long years to pay it off) loan! I was out of the country when the board met and accepted the package.

When I was informed through an international tele-phone call, I asked "What is the interest rate?"

"Two points over prime—floating rate," my comptroller answered. Prime today is 9 percent, so that'll be 11 percent interest."

I quickly calculated that this would be a burden of $1 million a year in interest alone! And interest could rise! To accept this loan would maximize our risk! "I can't and won't go along with it," I said. "I'll exercise my veto powers as board chairman, if need be. We can't run that risk! We'll just have to go out and collect more gifts, inspire more peo-ple!"

That decision carried. Thank God! It put the pressure on us to raise money and pay cash! This was fortunate, because two years later the prime rate hit 21 percent! Our interest charges would have been $2.3 million a year. *That* would have made the Crystal Cathedral go bankrupt!

You're smart! Use Possibility Thinking and you will an-ticipate and reduce the risks! After all, you don't just want your own way; you want to succeed!

Positivize Your *ADDICTIONS!*

You really want to succeed with all your heart, right? You desire with a passion to make your dream turn out? This project has to be a success! Your determination to achieve is volcanic, explosive, waiting to erupt with massive energy. You have more than enough resources to match your moun-tain!

Then hear this—check your addictions. That's right, your private habits. We all have them. The human being is a creature of habits. That's okay. In fact this reality can be harnessed to work for us and contribute enormously to our follow-through behavior.

The point is: Are your addictions positive or negative? "Mixed," you say. Of course! So let's go to work to clean up our act! Check your eating habits, exercise habits, sexual habits, reading habits, relaxation habits. I don't need to preach a sermon to you, do I? I respect your intelligence too much to insult you by telling you what's right and what's wrong. My job is to alert you to the positive possibilities of positive addictions!

Had I not been motivated to eradicate the negative addiction of tobacco out of my life, I might have died of lung cancer. I was officiating at the marriage of Glenn Ford in his Beverly Hills home. Jimmy Stewart, Frank Sinatra, John Wayne, Bill Holden, the groom, and I were gathered in relaxed conversation. Sinatra lit up. "When you gonna quit smokin', Francis?" Wayne muttered.

"When did you quit, Duke?" Blue Eyes answered.

"When I decided I'd rather live than smoke!"

I was in my mid-forties when a church member pressed a loving finger in my softly ballooning middle and announced, "Reverend Schuller, you're still young enough to correct a potentially fatal problem!" Well, he appointed himself to be my trainer. After fifteen years of running, I realize I've developed a *positive* addiction. I can't quit! I'm hooked on it! I have no idea how often my mind has been cleared by my running—cleared for creative ideas that have made me successful!

Form positive addictions because negative addictions will destroy you as we have seen too many times.

He was an "up-and-coming" candidate for the top spot. He was determined, prepared, well-connected. What a network he had. At some time, he became first liberal, then cavalier, finally careless about satisfying his sexual needs. Rumor had it he was a "womanizer," not exactly the image for the person who would sit in the Big Chief's office. He denied the allegations. Then the scandal broke. His career was finished overnight. It was a bad deal—a lousy tradeoff!

Then there's the supersuccessful fellow who died too young. The paper listed the cause as pneumonia. Some of us who knew him (and failed in our efforts to help him extricate himself from his negative addictions) know he died of AIDS.

I'll never know how much of my success is due to my happy marriage. All of our life we've practiced safe sex.

That's "wait till you're married!" (We did.) Never violate your faithfulness with a single affair—not one isolated adventure. Then you're really safe from disease and from mental distractions on the job and from blackmail or extortion! The result? Positive sexual habits that contribute immeasurably to super success! Old fashioned? Well, that makes my values classical, not fashionable, which means that values that pass the test of time must be right after all.

Okay, it's your turn. Use Possibility Thinking to uncover and screen out negative addictions that could take you down a dead-end road!

Then form positive addictions. You do that when you (1) Sow a prayer; reap an idea. (2) Sow the idea; reap an action. (3) Sow the action; reap a habit. (4) Sow the habit; reap a reputation! (5) Sow the reputation; reap a destiny!

Finalize Your *PLANS!*

In the process of success you are now ready to wind up the preparations phase and head for the launching phase. You're the pilot. The plane is on the runway waiting for clearance from the tower. Review your check list.

1. Have you filed a flight plan? Do you know where you want to go?
2. Do you know how to get to your destination?
3. Are you in shape to "take her up"? Clear headed? Well rested?
4. Are you ready for problems? Do you have ideas on how you'll deal with them?
5. Have you checked the forecast? Is the climate right for you to take off now? Or would a delay be the wiser side of courage?
6. Review your prepared plans once more. Remember, (a) check, (b) double-check, (c) recheck. Listen to the old Russian tailor's proverb, "Measure three times but cut only once!"
7. Okay, all set? Let's go for it! *"Don't forego it; go for it,"* to quote my Possibility Thinking son, Robert Anthony Schuller.

Verbalize Your *EXPECTATIONS!*

Now is the time to take the plunge. Your expectations have been clarified. Much failure results from a confusion of expectations. Your dream is visualized clearly in your mind. Your goal has been lifted to the top of your priorities. You've done an immense amount of back-up work. Now it's time to move from Possibility Thinking to Possibility Talking!

Issue the news release. Call for a press conference. Place an ad in the paper. Move your dream out of the closet onto Main Street. This is the moment you've prayed for, dreamed about, studied and prepared for! You are on stage. It's your turn to speak. This moment has a name; it is called *commitment*! You announce your engagement to marry. You sign a lease for the store. You make out the application and place your nonrefundable check on the table. This is the point of no return. Scary? No! EXCITING! Tomorrow people will be talking about you!

Then comes the surprise: cards, calls, good wishes from people you never expected to support you! Strength and encouragement come from unexpected sources. Out of the blue people approach you! Are you surprised? Persons were waiting for a leader to emerge offering a product, a service, a dream that struck their fancy! You never know how many birds are in your neighborhood until you put out the bird feeders. You never know how many friends you have out there until you "Let Your Dream Fly!"

Congratulations! I'm proud of you. Now what? Well, you've given your word to the public—that's what! Integrity takes over. You will just have to make a go of it! It's amazing how much energy commitment taps and releases!

Actualize Your *DREAMS!*

Now, you're in for it! Success is waiting for you! It's waiting to see if you will follow through, hang in there, keep on keeping on paying the price in personal sacrifice to actualize your dream. From this point on you and only you can kill your dream. Your dream now has a life of its own. Only you can abort it. Others may frustrate you; that's to be expected. Envious and shortsighted people may obstruct you. But only one person has the authority to sign the death certificate of your God-inspired dream, and that person is you! But by this time you have too much invested—most importantly your credibility and integrity. You *can't* walk away from it.

"I have a dream." Remember? Dr. Martin Luther King, Jr., made those words famous. Coretta Scott King told me once in the Crystal Cathedral, "Martin himself was aware of the dangerous path he was treading. Yet he believed that his commitment to his Lord and to his fellow human beings was the way of Christ. He knew that people who have made that commitment have usually been sacrificed."

And so he was killed. But that didn't stop the movement! *Success is never ending!*

What was the secret of his success? Total commitment to make that dream come true at any price. "I think," Coretta said, "through the process of self-dedication and total commitment, you inspire a lot of people and you can cause change to take place within the lives of people."

Few invitations to preach or speak have come to me that I was more honored to accept than when Dr. King's widow asked me to preach the sermon in the Ebenezer Baptist Church in Atlanta on her husband's birthday celebration in January 1987. "Martin Luther King, Jr., can be called a Possibility Thinker who knew how to make his dream come true," I said. "How do you actualize your dreams?" I asked that prestigious congregation.

"I am!

"I can!

"I will!

"That's how!" I said.

"*I am.* I am somebody. I am a child of God. I am a friend of Jesus Christ. I may be illiterate or untutored, but I am somebody! God can give me His dreams to carry out and fulfill, and I believe He has! I am God's chance to do this wonderful thing! Don't ask me why God picks, so often, the unknown, the unheralded, to do the impossible! A peasant girl in Nazareth to bear Jesus in her womb. A peasant girl from Yugoslavia to become Mother Teresa. The list in history is endless."

"Where did you get your dream?" I asked Coretta King.

She responded, "It was while I was attending Antioch College, founded by Horace Mann, that I heard the quotation that deeply motivated me. Horace Mann said to his first graduating class at Antioch in the late 1850s, 'Be ashamed to die until you've won some victory for humanity.'"

So there are no great people—the so-called great people only heard, lived by, and often died for the dream that consumed them!

"*I can!*

"If I am God's chance to bear this dream to full life, then *I can*! For He is more interested in the success of this divine possibility than I am! And 'God who has begun this good work in me will complete it!' So I can do this beautiful thing through Christ who strengthens me!

"*I will!*

"I am! I can! I will actualize my dream.

"I will press ahead.

"I will settle down and see it through.

"I will solve the problems.

"I will pay the price.

"I will never walk away from my dream until I see my dream walk away: Alert! Alive! Achieved!"

Maximize Your RESULTS!

Do you remember Level Ten of a dream? You are there now, at the danger point. "The *is* must never catch up with the *ought*," Dr. Victor Frankl wisely taught. I once wrote a whole book on this subject. I called it, *The Peek-to-Peak Principle*. Once you have reached the mountaintop, don't stop! Until every hungry person in the world is fed; every crying person is comforted; every depressed person has cause to smile again; every discouraged person is encouraged; and every lethargic person is motivated—don't stop possibilitizing.

"To whom much is given, from him much will be required," Jesus taught (Luke 12:48). Success carries with it a wonderfully heavy responsibility to use this new power as a lever to shift the world a little closer to God! Now is the time not to luxuriate, vegetate, or procrastinate, but to dedicate!

Now you have a power base. Use it! Now you have influence. Wield it! Now you have success. Share it! On the peak catch a peek—a new vision, a new dream, a loftier goal! Don't stop at the top!

Colonize Your *SUCCESS!*

So, where do you go from "up"? Why, you now use your base as a launching platform! When our television ministry succeeded from 1970 to 1971, we branched out to televise in New York, Chicago, and Philadelphia. After five years we added more "colonies" in a dozen other cities. We only expanded as the new colonies became self-supporting. We never fell into the tempting trap to borrow money to "go national fast"! Today we have nearly two hundred outlets.

If you have succeeded, then colonize your success. If you stop where you are now, if you fail to continue to grow, then you will begin to die.

Colonize your success! If you have succeeded—build on it! Use your success on a small scale to branch out carefully! Not too fast! Nor too slow!

The business world and Wall Street have been amazed at the growth of a company called Wal-Mart. Wal-Mart is a discount store that opened in Arkansas in 1962. When the company went public in 1970, an original investment in one hundred shares sold for about $1,650. It would be worth more than $700,000 today!

The founder and chairman, Sam Walton, has capitalized on his success to such an extent that *Time* magazine in May of 1987 called him "America's richest man."

Yet Sam Walton lives modestly, drives a Ford pickup, and delivers donuts to the loading-dock crew or helps a clerk approve a personal check.

Wal-Mart opened its first store in 1962. Sam Walton

capitalized on the principles that made that store a success and in turn incorporated them into new stores until he had a chain across the country, making his company the fourth largest U.S. retailer.

He has done it by giving the public what they want—low prices with no frills. And he has developed a loyal following from his 151,000 employees with whom the ideas and the profits are freely shared. Many of the best ideas have come from the bottom up. And because of the open policy, the stores keep changing thousands of little things that make a world of difference in the end.

So have you succeeded?! Then "pro-seed" with your success. Pro-seed is short for profit-seed. Pour your profits back into the business as seeds for expansion. The possibilities are tremendous!

Revitalize Your *IMAGINATION!*

By now, my Possibility Thinking friend, you are ready to connect with the ultimate power source that can continue to stimulate and sustain your success.

"What is that?" you ask. I answer with a long question: What power in the world—

- *Travels* faster than the speed of light?
- *Penetrates* all known barriers, whether steel or granite?
- *Transcends time,* both past and future, enabling a person to roll the clock and calendar backward for centuries or forward into infinity?
- *Transports* a human consciousness and awareness instantaneously across continents and cultures to hear sounds, see sights, and breathe in exotic fragrances of intoxicating perfumes?
- *Provides* a tantalizing glimpse of eternity and immortality now, exposing the possibility that ultimate aliveness is living without having to transport this baggage of bones, flesh, hair, and blood?
- *Supplies humans* with a seminal source of creativity: splashing oils on canvas to create a masterpiece; mix-

ing notes, tunes, and melodies until a masterful musical composition evolves; conceiving dreams in the minds of ordinary humans of all ages until a common person is caught up, grabs ahold, and really gets into a fantastic goal and an exciting, consuming project?

- *Programs data* into the subconscious which calculates breakthrough solutions to what were impossible deadlocks and unsolvable problems?
- *Transforms the mental climate* in a social unit until an awkward, tense, embarrassing emotional environment is suddenly relaxed, easy, and pleasant?
- *Sharpens* the focus of human attention to needlelike precision until the basketball goes whoosh through the hoop, the baseball cuts an incredible curve across the plate, the football soars, a perfect kick through the goal posts?
- *Combines internal contradictions creatively* until irreconcilable differences are surprisingly bridged by constructive compromises?

What is this force? What is this incredible power? This power which ignites creative fires in the hearts of Possibility Thinkers is called IMAGINATION.

And is it truly available to every living human being, regardless of economic or social standing? The answer is yes! I could tell you stories of untutored, unlettered, illiterate members of the most remote tribes from the internal mountain country of New Guinea, in the South Pacific, to the heartland of Africa who have experienced and harnessed this absolutely immeasurable, immense power!

Claim this remarkable, miraculous gift and you will be able to see a thing before it is. Why, this is a divine quality! It may well be the most impressive evidence of the reality of God coming to live and flow constructively and creatively through human beings! This could be the proof of the biblical teaching that "Man is created in the *image* of God."

"Imageofgodinus" is the way I write the word "imagination"! Yes, imagination is the "image-of-God-in-us"! Like a window, it can sparkle clear and clean, allowing a clear vision to the horizon. Or it can be covered with a film, thin at first; then slowly, imperceptibly, a thickening layer of sediment accumulates on the defenseless glass until the sparkling mirror quality of this window of the soul, where God shines through, is darkened and dulled, distorting the picture. Fatigue, frustration, failures, and fears soil this screen where God wants to project a clear readout of his programming for our lives!

So revitalize your imagination! And a darkened mind will light up in technicolor! Action! Sound! Energy! Enthusiasm! Drive! Determination! Zeal! Zest! Vitality!

Now look what happens to the person whose imagination is revitalized! The window is washed. The screen is cleared, the projection sharply focused. Suddenly fears are wiped out. The darkness is washed away. The brightly glowing vision appears on the mind's inner screen. An inexplicable surge of overpowering determination to strive and succeed energizes the taproot of human motivation. You are hooked on a happy goal! Nobody can stop you now. You see the vision clearly. You catch an unmistakable picture of the dream that God sketched for your life. You're a dancing teenager again. You're a budding Olympic contender. You're an up-and-coming achiever. "Watch out, world, here I come."

Imagination, what an amazing channel of immeasurable spiritual power! Imagination—it's the audio and visual channel that God uses to communicate His dreams to your consuming consciousness. Wow! When your imagination is turned on, you are *really alive.* No chemical or drug can produce a high comparable to this healthy, holy high. But turn off this imagination and allow the screen to become dark and you are suddenly bored, dull, and boring—and terribly vulnerable to an unholy host of potentially destructive stimuli that seek to fill your inner emotional vacuum and satisfy your heart's craving for excitement.

Success? It does not happen without a total aliveness generated only by a revitalized imagination. The developer imagines the structures rising—with fountains, steel, glass, escalators, and elevators!

The student imagines the graduation day: cap and gown, a degree and a diploma in his hand.

The father and mother imagine a home of their own. They clip pictures out of magazines. They pore over illustrations of furniture. They look at baby furniture and children's clothes and imagine a family!

The salesman imagines the faces of his customers lighting up with excitement to buy his product and service because it's just what they need.

The communicator imagines his audience in rapt attention drinking in his message and applauding the performance.

The surgeon imagines the sharp, smooth incision. What skill and grace!

The teacher imagines the students as tall, mature adults who are successful contributors to a healthy society!

The author imagines his article in print. He sees the book with his picture on the jacket! He can't wait to get started.

The manager imagines defensive faces of workers changing shape to become receptive, welcoming and appreciating and accepting his supervision.

The financier imagines a small dollar base growing larger, slowly, then a bit faster, then pyramiding, until, with incredible speed, his resources multiply and his fortunes inflate! He is now positioned for joyous philanthropy!

The athlete imagines her body responding to exercise and fitness routines until the mirror reflects an amazing profile! Now she imagines running swiftly, like an elk, like a greyhound, like a fox. She imagines jumping over the wall— high, higher—clearing the bar, breaking the limit! Bells ring. The applause is deafening. She did it. She really did it!

Success is never ending and failure is never final to that person who knows how to revitalize and renew the God-given powers of creative imagination.

How do we revitalize imagination? There are many ways. Study the timeless wisdom found in the Bible. Read inspiring stories in magazines and on the sports and business pages of the newspaper. Observe and experience what is around you, and you will see countless living illustrations of great and wonderful achievements being racked up by people just like you! Let their accomplishments inspire your imagination!

Now draw close to successful persons and people and know that if they can do it, you can too!

How do you revitalize your imagination? I asked this question to a friend who is extremely creative. His answer was, "My imagination is rekindled and renewed when I relate to people who really respect me and build me up." So you revitalize your imagination by revitalizing your relationships. Draw close to Possibility Thinking persons who see the potential within you and honestly affirm your value and worth. As you receive and respect their affirming compliments, you'll begin to believe in yourself too!

So begin by revitalizing your relationship with the one person who always builds you up and never puts you down. His name is Jesus Christ. Pray. Simply close your eyes. Talk to Him. Be quiet and give Him a chance to speak to you. Ask Him simple and sincere questions. Sit quietly and wait for answers. Give Him a chance to draw a picture in your imagination of the wonderful, holy, positive things He'd like you to do and be. Embrace His vision! Relish this divine delicacy of inspired and sanctified imagination. Feast on this inspiration from God that can and will become reality. Christ's power is actually evident in your life through imagination! There's no telling how far you will go now!

I Don't Believe in . . .
Luck!

I Believe in . . .
Pluck!

P.S.: . . . . Plus Prayer
and Planning!

PART II

. . . *Failure is Never Final!*

CHAPTER 7

Where Do You Go from "Out"?

*I*t was 1985. I stood before the most talented, gifted, and accomplished young women in the country. We were gathered in Mobile, Alabama, for the Junior Miss contest. I had been asked to speak to the girls competing in the national competition. They had come from every state and represented our country's finest young women.

I looked across that sea of lovely young faces and wondered who would be chosen the next Junior Miss of America. The next day the cameras and the newspapers would carry the news of the winner to the entire country. The nation would remember the winner, but what about the losers? They had come so far, but only one would stand in the winner's circle. All the others would be OUT!

I was concerned for them all—those who would lose and the one who would win. The ones who would not receive the crown might feel they had failed! And the winner would wear her crown for a year, then pass it on to someone else. Then she, too, would be OUT! Where would these lovely, gifted, ambitious young women go from "out"? Would they be bitter? Would they be disillusioned? Would they be so intimidated that they would never try again?

I felt that the best gift I could give these girls would be a clear perspective of who they were and what they had accomplished. I wanted to give them the reassurance that they were all special!

I began, "Tomorrow night only one girl will be chosen as the Junior Miss of America. Only one will walk away with the title. Only one will wear the crown. So tonight I have a question that I want you to think about carefully. The question is this: '*Where do you go from OUT?*'

"A lot of people all over the world feel they're 'out' of something or other. They're not asked to join the clubs. Or they fail to get an invitation to a party. They are overlooked for promotions or awards. Some people are living on a high-class street; others are not. Some are rich and some are poor. Some have it and some don't. Everybody is out of something or some circle. Tomorrow night one person will be in the winning circle—the rest of you will be out. And if you happen to be 'out' and not 'in,' join the human race!

"In the Scriptures it says, 'For you shall go out with joy,/ And be led forth with peace'" (Isa. 55:12).

I continued, "If you don't win you can return home with joy and be led forth with peace if you can remember that you are ALL winners! You are all successful! The truth is that even those who try but don't make it are winners too.

"The losers are those who never dared to try because they were afraid they wouldn't make it. Most people fail because they haven't tried. And they haven't tried because they don't want to run the risk of being disappointed. Those who try have already succeeded in a very important area of life, for they have conquered the fear of failure. As soon as you sign up, decide to go for it and give it a shot. You are a winner! You haven't let the threat of a possible disappointment keep you from trying to do something great.

"For years I've kept these words on the wall of my office: '*I'd rather attempt to do something great and fail, than attempt to do nothing and succeed.*'

"Nobody who has tried is really OUT! You may feel out of it. You may feel you have failed. You may be bitterly disappointed and disillusioned. But these are distortions. The reality is that you are a part of the winner's circle. You are a part of the elite group of people who tried!

"The person who wins the number one spot will be surprised how quickly others will forget her success unless she reminds them. Fame is fleeting. Fortunes can be dissipated overnight.

"It means we all have to learn how to make exits gracefully. We can all learn a lot from the lesson my mother taught me when I was a little boy. Before a piano recital, she would say, 'Rehearse the opening again. Now, rehearse the ending again.' When I protested, she replied, 'Listen, Bob, make your opening terrific. Make your ending glorious. If you do, your audience will forget the mistakes in the middle!' Learn to live so that your exit is gracious."

Make Your Exit Gracious

Every year, at the beginning of the new year, national magazines and newspapers have "in" and "out" lists. These lists tell which foods are in, which foods are out; which fashions are in, which fashions are out; which entertainers are in, which entertainers are out; which politicians are in, which politicians are out.

Like the beauty contestants, the fashion designers, the entertainers, and the politicians, we will all at one time or another face exits. We will all be suddenly, unexpectedly OUT!

- You thought your career was progressing fine, that you'd be tapped as the president of the company. How many years did you give to the corporation? And then the crucial decision was made to bring somebody in from the outside and to pass you by. You're out. *Where do you go from out?*
- You thought you had read the market so well. You placed a huge order. It's in the warehouse. Suddenly, the fickle styles change, fashions pass, and the orders

don't come in. That product is out. *Where do you go from out?*

- You had a big hit and made a name for yourself. Suddenly you can't get a decent contract, a solid booking, a great script, or a really good song. The promoters don't want you anymore. You're out. *Where do you go from out?*
- Your spouse is no longer with you, removed perhaps by death, maybe through divorce. Now you're out. *Where do you go from out?*
- Your future was secure. Everything was unfolding as planned. Everything was going great. Then an unexpected pain. The doctor calls. You've got cancer. *Where do you go from out?*

All of us are going out—sometime, some way, somewhere. The question is not *Will I have to make an exit?* but rather *How will I make my exit?*

When you go out—from success to failure, from failure to success, from health to sickness, from job to retirement, from marriage to singleness, from life to death—what kind of an attitude will you have? The spirit of your exit is all-important, for it will affect your reputation as well as whether or not you will enjoy the rest of your journey.

Some go out with bitterness, anger, hurt, pain, and self-pity. They are jealous of those who are still in. They leave behind a bad impression because they are now in a self-inflicted position of weakness.

On the other hand some people go out with *joy*! These people turn their exits into entrances. They operate from a position of strength rather than weakness, simply because they have adopted a positive outlook toward their "failure" or their exit.

As a pastor and a counselor I have made it my business to study people. I have seen some people overwhelmed by tragedy, while I have seen the positive attitude of others overwhelm their tragedy. These are undergoers who became overcomers. I have counseled with superstars who watched their stellar careers slide on the skids. "They tell me I no longer have box-office appeal." Some have handled it very graciously. Others? Well, many drink too much.

I have counseled with farmers from my home state who have lost the family farm. The auction at the courthouse was horrendously painful. The land and the buildings had been passed on from great-grandfather who came from the "old country." Now they're OUT! The title to the land is recorded in a strange new name. Their keys are turned in.

OUT! Fired? Divorced? Separated? Parting of the ways? OUT! Death? Bankruptcy? Lost your lease? Sudden shifts in the market? Oh, how many exits there are in this pavilion called Life on Planet Earth!

Remember: *Success is never ending; failure is never final!* Healing may and must be found in two stages. Stage One is Damage Control. Stage Two is Renewal and Recovery.

Stage One: Damage Control

You are out! Shocked that this could ever happen to you. Surprised that you are surviving it, barely. If anyone had ever told you you'd be going through this, you couldn't have believed it. And if they had told you that you would survive it, you couldn't have believed that either!

But you hurt as you've never hurt before.

Learn some lessons now from the veterans who have had a lot of experience enduring, tolerating, and absorbing pain. Here's how they patch up the ragged hole. To stop the hemorrhaging of their life spirits, they employ front-line, damage control therapy: "Just get the poor fellow home alive. He'll recover. Right now let's contain the loss and control the rapidly spreading hurt."

So listen and learn from the scarred soldiers. How did they pass through? What advice do they offer?

1. *Keep a sense of humor.* It's no sacrilege to laugh at a funeral! It can release tremendous tension. Morticians, medical doctors, pastors, soldiers have all learned to laugh or the grief would kill them! Jokes are important. Welcome them!

2. *Accept and receive the comfort offered.* Reject and resist the temptation to rebuff the condolences and encouragement well-meaning people offer. You need "strokes." Take them.

3. *Draw close—don't pull away—from your closest circle of family and friends.* They're going to help you. Be cooperative. Your "folks" really love you. Remember, *Hope isn't the absence of suffering. It is living in the presence of love!*

4. *Work hard at holding the rest of your life together.* Be careful. Grief could tear the rest of your life apart! I've seen a young couple lose a child and allow this tragedy to wreck their marriage too. I've seen an executive fired in a corporate power play. A spoke was knocked out of the wheel of his life. His attitude was negative: "What the ____!" Angry, he kicked the rest of the spokes out too. Wife! Family! Health! Religion! "Wait a minute," I pleaded in vain. "You need whatever spokes you have left! There are enough spokes remaining in your wheel of fortune to take you along the road until you can find a repair shop. Right now, let's control the damage. Take care of the spokes you have left! Ride on them."

When You are Suddenly OUT, You Will Need Your Sense of HUMOR.

When you can see something light and funny in your situation, then you can be gracious in your loss.

When my wife, Arvella, had her breast removed for cancer and when my daughter, Carol, lost her leg in a motorcycle accident, they made some pretty funny jokes about their situations. In fact, one day Arvella and Carol both joked about their unusual day of shopping. Now it's not uncommon for mothers and daughters to go shopping together. But there are few mothers and daughters who have gone to the same store for their spare parts. Arvella and Carol spent the day being fitted—not for dresses, but for prosthetics! They made up quite a few jokes about it, which were very healing. Never underestimate the power of laughter and humor.

Henry Viscardi knows how much healing love and laughter can bring when you are OUT. Henry was born in 1912 in New York City, the son of immigrant parents. He was born without normal legs. He spent most of his early life in a hospital. He did not receive his artificial limbs, with which he walks today, until he was twenty-seven years old. But what a life he has lived!

He has become one of the world's most respected figures in the fields of rehabilitation and education. He has devoted his life to ensuring that severely-disabled individuals might have all of the opportunities to achieve their fullest potential as human beings, and he's always believed that living proof is the most persuasive.

In 1952 Henry founded the internationally-famed Human Resources Center in Elbertson, Long Island, and through the center's research and training institutes, Abilities, Inc., and Human Resources School, he has demonstrated to the world that the disabled can be fully integrated into every phase of American life.

Henry has been an advisor to every president from Franklin Roosevelt to Ronald Reagan. His honors and awards are many. He is highly respected and admired across the country and is well known for his positive attitude and his endearing sense of humor.

When I interviewed him at the Crystal Cathedral one spring morning, he looked at the audience of over three thousand people and said, "Many of you may be impressed by the the fact that I'm standing here on two artificial limbs. But that, after all, is not a handicap; it's only an inconvenience. Has it occurred to you that here it is almost Easter Sunday, and I haven't changed my socks since the Fourth of July?! But—I hope *you* have!"

I asked him, "Henry, where did you get such a positive attitude toward life?" I shall never forget his answer.

"I suppose I got it from my parents. I remember asking my mother when I was a child, 'Of all to be so born, why me?' And in her simple peasant wisdom, my mother replied, 'When it was time for another crippled boy to be born in the world, the Lord and His counselors held a meeting to decide where he should be sent, and the Lord said, *I think the Viscardis would be a good family for a crippled boy.'*

"And so I feel a great deal of gratitude today—for America, this great land in which we live, which gave me an opportunity to become a learned man, operating in difficult fields. In any other land I probably would have been lucky to wind up selling lottery tickets on some street corner or counting gasoline drums on some loading dock. God bless America for what it's given me!"

That positive attitude and sense of humor carried Henry Viscardi when he was OUT. Now he is using that same humor to help handicapped children who are considered OUT. He has built a school for the disabled and is educating them because, as he said, "No matter how disabled a child may be born, if that boy or girl becomes a learned man or woman, then they're no longer disabled."

Today, in his Human Resources School, there are one hundred and fifty students from six months of age (with their mothers) through high school. As educated men and women in this highly sophisticated world, they will be prepared to face life's challenges and become self-sufficient, dignified individuals.

Henry commented, "These students are not ordinary people seeking extraordinary destinies, but these wonderful students of ours are extraordinary people seeking *ordinary* destinies—to love and be loved, to be the same and not different from the rest of the world, as they are in the eyes of God. And it's a place of great humor if you ever come to it. If you were to visit the school, you would find laughter throughout the campus.

"I shall never forget the time when a group of little ones invited me to a tea. I sat and waited for the tea. Finally, one little girl came in pushing the tea caddy, and her teacher said, somewhat annoyed, 'You're late; we've been waiting for the tea. What kept you?' The little girl replied, 'I couldn't find the tea strainer.'

"I should have let it go at that, but I said to her, 'What did you do?' And she said, 'I used the fly swatter!' I had to drink the tea! But I haven't enjoyed a cup since!"

Henry Viscardi has a wonderful wife, Lucille, four daughters, and eight grandchildren. All of them stand by him in his dreams and his aspirations. He has pledged that as long as there is but one disabled American who prefers the challenges of life to a sheltered existence, he will devote his energies to that person's need.

Henry concluded his visit to the Crystal Cathedral with this statement: "My friends, to hope is a duty, not a luxury. To hope is to turn dreams into reality. Blessed are those who dream dreams and are willing to pay the price to make them come true."

You can go OUT with joy—if you have some jokes and a positive attitude to carry you UP and BEYOND!

When You Are Suddenly OUT, You Will Need Some STROKES.

We all need comfort at times, so don't be afraid to admit it if you are hurting. The saddest thing in the world is that there are hurting people who won't let anybody know how they feel—not even their wives, their husbands, their families, their pastors, or their friends. *If you're too proud to admit you're hurting, don't be surprised if nobody seems to care.*

Loving, caring, positive strokes can do wonders to give you the strength to make your exit graciously and the courage to make a new grand entrance. The power of carefully chosen words should never be minimized. Strokes can be very healing when you are suddenly OUT!

One woman, Patti Lewis, knows how devastating it can be to be OUT after forty years of marriage to the celebrated comedian, Jerry Lewis. After bearing and raising six sons, she suddenly found herself OUT.

Patti, who has always been a Christian, says that her relationship with the Lord and friendships with other women helped carry her through. The loving strokes from these women were so helpful that Patti and Jackie Joseph, who had been married to the actor Ken Berry, started a local organization that they call LADIES, which stands for "Life After Divorce Is Eventually Sane."

This group is composed of women who were married to famous men. As Patti said, "Let's face it. You see their faces in the paper all the time, and it's not easy to maintain your sanity. It's difficult to remember that you are special when your self-esteem is shattered through a divorce. You cry all the time, you become very bitter, and you can't sleep. But when you can feel anger, then you're on the road to recovery.

"Anger is the last stage and when you get to that point, suddenly the skies seem to open up and happiness floods in again."

I asked, "Patti, are you still bitter toward Jerry?"

Her reply was quick and sure. "Oh, no! I bear no malice. In fact we are friends. But I don't know if I could have gotten to this place if it weren't for the prayers and encouragement and loving advice that I received in my small group of LADIES."

You can go OUT with joy if you have some loving STROKES!

When You Are Suddenly OUT, You Will Need Some FOLKS to Stand By You.

I have observed that people who make gracious exits and glorious entrances are those who have friends, family, or loved ones to give them vital emotional support, encouragement, and guidance.

In the famous play *Anastasia* we meet the woman who claims to be the daughter of the czar who somehow has escaped death during the Bolshevik revolution. She is discovered alone in an insane asylum where she was kept after her failed attempt to jump from a bridge into a raging river. She is despondent, depressed, and without a family or friends.

Then one of the doctors comes across a newspaper clipping that sparks a whole new life, a whole new beginning for this lost soul. In the clipping he sees a remarkable likeness to Anastasia, the lost daughter of the czar of Russia. Through hypnosis he hears his patient describe the reprehensible assassination of Anastasia's family. She seemingly knows details of Anastasia's past that only the princess would know.

And so the mystery begins. Those who believe in Anastasia compile irrefutable evidence that she is the missing princess. Those who doubt and suspect her of fraud discover just as much evidence against her.

However, her "Grandmother," the Empress, chooses to believe in Anastasia. Anastasia begins to shed the trampled, defeated persona and adopts a regal stance. She blooms. She stands straight and tall and moves with grace. The withered young woman from the insane asylum blossoms into a princess.

What inspired the transformation? How did Anastasia find her way out and up? She says in the play, "You must understand that it never mattered whether or not I was a princess. It only matters that I am I, that someone, if it be only one, has held out their arms to welcome me back from death."[1]

You can go OUT from any situation if you have someone who believes in you. And you can go UP and BEYOND if you have someone who cares for you and cheers you on.

Lou Little was football coach at Georgetown University. The college president came to him one day and, naming a student, said, "Lou, do you know this fellow?"

"Sure," Lou answered. "He's been on my squad four years. I've never played him. He's good enough, but he's just not motivated."

"Well," the president continued, "we just heard that his father died. Will you break the news to him?"

The coach put his arm around the young man in a back room and told him about his father. "I'm very sorry, son. Take a week off."

But the next day the coach was amazed to see the student in the locker room suiting up for the game. "What are you doing here?" Little inquired.

"Tonight's the big game. I've got to play in it."

"But you know I've never started you."

---

[1]Marcelle Maurette, *Anastasia* (New York: Random House, 1954), 161.

"Start me tonight, and you won't be sorry," the moist-eyed player stated firmly.

Softening, the coach decided that if he won the toss he would use him on the first play. He couldn't do that much damage on the kickoff return. Georgetown won the toss. On the first play this fatherless boy came tearing down the field with the ball like a tornado. Coach Little, shocked, left him in for another play and then another. He blocked; he tackled; he passed; he ran. He literally won the ball game for Georgetown University that day.

In the locker room Coach Little, perplexed, asked, "Son, what happened?"

The happy, perspiring victor said, "Coach, you never knew my dad, did you? Well, Sir, he was blind, and today was the first time he ever saw me play."[1]

You can go OUT and UP with joy if you have FOLKS who believe in you. The truth is that we all have folks. We all have friends. We all have someone, somewhere, who cares about us and believes that we can make a comeback.

When You Are Suddenly OUT, You Will Need Some SPOKES to Keep Your Life Together.

You can go out with joy if you will guard the rest of your values against the possibility of suffering damage from what's happening. When you move from one passage in life to another, when you leave one era of your life completely behind you never to return, do not leave behind the ideals, the values, the morals, and the ethics.

Maybe you're single, through death or divorce. This does not now give you the liberty to forsake your morals and ideals. Maybe you've been passed by for a promotion or perhaps you're out looking for a job. This doesn't free you from the ethical restraints by which you've lived.

There must be abiding, eternal, spiritual values around which your life will continue to move. These are the spokes

---

[1]Robert Schuller, *Power Ideas for a Happy Family* (Old Tappan, New Jersey: Revell, 1971), 77, 78.

on the wheel of spiritual values from which you should never depart.

I am reminded of the time when my daughter, Sheila, auditioned for her high school musical. Sheila had done a lot of solo work in her school, so we encouraged her to audition for the lead. She even was approached by the drama teacher who pulled her aside and asked if she planned to audition. She said, "Sheila, there's a part in this show that is perfect for you. Take a script home and read it over this weekend and let me know what you think."

Sheila was naturally excited and flattered that the teacher had singled her out. She nearly floated home, script in hand. And the minute she stepped in the door, she retreated to her room, dreaming of stardom.

The role that her teacher had in mind for her, the comic lead, at first looked wonderful—charming, witty, and vivacious. But then Sheila came to a scene that deeply troubled her. Her character was to meet a handsome stranger, take him home with her and, in a light and funny scene, seduce him. It was a scene totally alien to Sheila's values.

Sheila didn't feel comfortable playing the role because everyone at school knew what her values were, and she knew the role would compromise her beliefs. As Sheila told me later, she put the script aside, bowed her head, and prayed, "Dear Lord, I want to be a success—for YOU! I want Your love to shine through. I want to be what You want me to be. Help me to do that, and show me how."

Sheila shared her concerns with us and explained that she wouldn't be auditioning for the role. She had decided to audition for the romantic lead instead.

That afternoon she filled out her audition card and indicated which part she wanted. She carefully omitted the name of the comic lead. However, when her teacher called her up to read, she told her to turn to a certain page in the script and read the part of the comic lead. Her teacher had already cast her in the role. Sheila's face grew hot with hurt and anger. In front of fifty other students and a panel of teachers, she said as calmly as she could, "I'm not auditioning for that role."

"Why not?" the teacher demanded. "It's an excellent part!"

"It's not right for me. I do not feel that as a professing Christian I can play that role."

"Sheila, I asked you to read the part. Now are you going to read or not?"

She could see that the only way to convince her teacher that she was not right for the role would be to read for her. So she read—as slowly and as monotonously as she could. Her teacher knew her capabilities as an actress, and she could see that Sheila was deliberately reading poorly. Since the other teachers were witnesses to her pitiful performance, the teacher would be forced to give the role to another girl.

Sheila handed the script back to her stunned teacher. Then she walked out of the auditorium with her head held high. She no sooner got out of the auditorium, however, than she felt tremendous disappointment. She ran to the parking lot where I was waiting. Flinging open the car door she cried, "Oh Dad! I didn't get the romantic lead. She never intended for me to read it. She was dead set that I do the comic lead."

Then she recounted the whole scene for me. Bitter tears streaked her face as she asked, "Why did she do that to me in front of all those kids?"

I took my darling daughter in my arms and said, "Oh, Sheila, God allowed it to happen so that you could make a statement of faith. I am so proud of you. God chose you to play an exceptional part today! He chose you out of all the other students to share in a loving way that Jesus is Lord of your life."

Then I looked her squarely in the eye and continued, "This afternoon, you were a smashing success! You get rave reviews from God and me!"

Imagine my further pride, when later Sheila was chosen out of all the other students in her school to sing "O Holy Night" for the annual Christmas show.

Sheila was able to make her exit graciously in the musical. She sang in the chorus and cheerfully supported the production, even though she was not in a position of prominence. Then she was able to make a glorious entrance on the "O Holy Night" solo.

Make Your Entrance Glorious!

You can make your exit gracious and your new entrance grand if you can look beyond, if you can keep in mind that failure is never final! And success is never ending!

I have the opportunity to get to know many different people. Most of them are ordinary people like you and me, but some are celebrities.

I count it a great privilege to have met and talked one-on-one with Sammy Davis, Jr. I had the chance to ask him questions about himself and about his attitude toward his life, his dreams, and his success. Sammy's trials are all pretty well known and documented by the press. His road to success was not always smooth.

When he first started out, he faced criticism and had to overcome a lot of barriers. He said, "Sometimes you get on that road and you're driven by those particular good thoughts but you take it just that one step too far and you're anxious to get there. The devil of success is right there on your shoulder now that you've got a taste of it, and he keeps saying, 'You can get more, you can get more, you can get more.' And you want more 'cause that's the name of our business. The bigger you are, the better you are. You ask yourself questions such as, 'How come I'm not making more money? How come I haven't gotten this?'

"So then I started to blame all of my personal theatrical failures on the fact that I was black. I figured that's why I didn't get it. Part of that was true. But a great part of it was not.

"I haven't the faintest idea as to where that zeal for more came from, but I know now that when I walk on the stage I no longer have those devils on me. I can walk out and have the kind of rapport with an audience regardless of race, color, creed 'cause I don't base it on that. I just base it on people to people. You know, in the old days I'd watch a television show and when they'd pan the audience I would count how many black people were in it. Now I just see people."

I asked Sammy, "Where did you get your inspiration when you were starting out? Did you have any role models?"

"Well, if you listen to me sing that song, 'Mr. Bojangles,' that will give you a clue, because I knew that kind of black minstrel. He was a street performer with a frayed collar and the frayed cuff, but he always kept himself immaculate in spite of his frayedness, and the hat was always cocked. But he was one of these men who had known disappointment and heartbreak of one kind or another. These were the men who never made it. But they were responsible for being an inspiration to young kids like myself."

"So you broke through the barriers; you were doing well when, suddenly, in 1954 you had your accident," I said.

"Yes. That accident should have killed me. All it took was my eye. Amazingly, the traumatic shock of it didn't hit me until two years after. I had worn a patch about a year when Humphrey Bogart said to me, 'Take the patch off. Do you want to be remembered as the best performer people have ever seen or as the guy with the patch?'

"So I took the patch off. Within that year I made three movies with the artificial eye. And I thank the good Lord because He used me as an instrument. I've had people tell me that they had an accident that took an eye, but they didn't let it stop them. They said they found inspiration from the way I handled my loss. I still hear that to this day, which makes me feel very good."

Sammy Davis, Jr., knows what it feels like to be suddenly OUT. When he had his accident he was forced to make an exit, which he made graciously. He kept his sense of humor. Jokes kept him going. He accepted comfort from friends like Frank Sinatra—strokes helped. And there were other folks, his fans. "Spokes"—he didn't kick them. He used them to ride on! So he was able to make a grand new, glorious entrance—bigger and better than before. Sammy learned to turn his entertaining into inspiration.

We are all, at one time or another, going to be OUT,

abandoned, thrown to the wind. But we can go OUT with joy if we will remember this: Every end is a new beginning!

So success is never ending! What appears to be failure is an illusion. Actually, failure is only a transition phase in the process of success.

All of your past is still a part of you! Your past successes continue to bear more fruit than you'll ever know. Many years ago I counseled a special person. It was the beginning of a warm friendship. After a few years all communication was abruptly halted, and not by me! I wasn't "in." Now I was suddenly "out." I felt I had been a success but now had become a failure.

"Not so," a wise associate pointed out. "You ministered to him during a phase of his life. You helped him get through it. Now he's on his own and spiritually strong. You haven't stopped succeeding because he doesn't need you anymore! In fact your success is *ongoing in him, for he is going on* without you!"

Yes, one single success has a way of keeping on blessing others who bless others! Success is never ending!

Stage Two: Renewal and Recovery

Now that the wound is dry and the scar tissue has formed, recovery is under way, and you know you still have a lot to give.

"Not long ago I ran out of the energy to keep being capable, busy, put-together and confident," wrote columnist Beclee Newcomer Wilson of her deep depression.

For her the battle was rough. Real. Understandable. Natural. Long. Too long. "There were trays of youthfully scrambled eggs brought to the bedside on tiptoe. The toast was heaped with real butter. There were no shoulds and oughts—the children were simply there. They brought true comfort defined as 'to strengthen, to invigorate, to cheer,'" Wilson wrote.

"When my depression lingered too long for them, they had their way to tell me. A rose had come on every tray.

'Mother,' Beth Anne declared one afternoon, 'you must stop. There are no more roses in the garden.'

"It was up to me. I had to find the power, the will for wholeness and healing."[2]

Get on with Dreaming Again.

Yes, to recover you must plan a comeback—find a new place to give yourself away!

How about joining a *Possibility Thinkers club*? There's one in your community. It may be a woman's club, a Rotary Club, a local church, a Bible study.

If you are coming from a setback, a bankruptcy, a personal or professional or financial "failure," then take a new look at those Possibility Thinkers. *Why are they "still hanging in there"?* How come they're not "out"? Decide to join them. Learn the tricks of their trade.

Possibility Thinkers Are WOW! Thinkers

Possibility Thinkers instinctively latch on to ideas that will catch on! I have never pursued a project unless my first reaction was, "WOW!" Intuitively, the subconscious releases a Freudian slip and judges the idea to be *outstanding*! Exceptional! Incredible! Fantastic! Beautifully possible!

Ideas that fail to generate such initial, immediate, positive impulses may lack the power to survive the energy-draining passages before fulfillment is realized. "Wow!"— the world must not be deprived of this accomplishment! The top prize goes to the idea or individual who has this one empowering imperative: PASSION!

Creative people have the ability to keep generating "Wow" ideas. Possibility Thinkers have developed and regularly deployed their own inventive tricks of the thinking trade. Let me share with you how to create "Wow" ideas!

---

[2]*Columbus Dispatch*, Sunday, July 29, 1979.

Think "Better"

Question: How can we do a better job than anyone else? How can we improve on our best performance? Someone will break our records—let that someone be us! Whatever we did right yesterday, tomorrow we'll do it better! How can we get smarter and wiser to become better than the best when we are the best? You're on your way to "Wow" power.

Think "Brighter"

The Possibility Thinker will see the bright side of what others see as only dark. "Look at it this way," the optimist says, pointing out an angle no one has considered.

I know a woman who was "out" but became "in" when she learned to look at the bright side. She married a serviceman who took her away from her cultured, stimulating social scene in a big eastern city. He was assigned, of all places, to a California desert post. His duties and his salary kept them confined to the base. The military personnel bored her. The local community? In her words, "only hicks and Indians." In deep depression, she wrote her mother that she couldn't stand it any longer. She was leaving her husband. She was coming home. She was going back to the university.

Her mother wrote back: "Two people live in the same prison. One sees bars; the other stars. Don't leave, Honey. Bloom where you're planted."

She cried. That night she took a walk and saw the stars as she had never seen them in Philadelphia! She went to the library and picked up a book on stars. A new consuming interest was born! She stopped to talk history and culture with a local Indian woman. The woman not only taught her the native arts and crafts but embraced her as one of their own. She was "in" again!

Someone asked me, "What do you do if people are *hopelessly* trapped?"

I said to my friend, "Well, then, you can at least give them hope. If they have hope, that tender little light will begin to burn a little tunnel and the tunnel becomes their escape to freedom."

Think brighter, and you'll tap into "Wow" power.

Think "Build"

Intuitively, Possibility Thinkers ask: "Will this be constructive? Will it *build* anything? A structure? A business? A character? A community spirit? Pride? An institution? A future? A great and honorable reputation? Will it build better goodwill? Will it build perpetuity or longevity? Will it build better relations—in race and religion?" If so, it has potential "Wow" power.

Think "Beauty"

Does the idea have sparkle? Beauty is practical, too! In fact it's hard to sell something that doesn't please the eye! Will your faith, your philosophy, your religion, your psychology produce "Beautiful Persons"? Mine does, and that's why I'm passionately sold on it.

Remember: "Wow Power" produces "Will Power"! So that's how to get back IN again.

Possibility Thinkers Are NOW! Thinkers

When a "Wow" opportunity, a "Wow" invitation, or a "Wow" idea comes to them, Possibility Thinkers snatch it!

"The early bird gets the worm." They know that! They are do-it-now people. They pick up the phone. They call for a get-together—"How soon can you make it?" They rearrange their previous plans to make time. Tomorrow is too late! Now is the time to seize the opportunity.

Today! Stop crying. Start possibilitizing. Begin, today, to get back "in" somewhere. The phone won't ring by itself for you; the letters won't just come to you. You have to get up, get out, and get with it!

Your greatest enemy is procrastination. Your biggest obstacle is inertia. Your most dangerous temptation is delaying. Getting started is the hardest part. Breaking loose and "beginning" is the toughest job. Postponing can wipe out the opportunity. Scratch out the word "someday." Someday is today!

Isn't it wonderful that you are going to make a brand new start?

Possibility Thinkers Are HOW! Thinkers

If the idea is a "Wow," then the questions of Possibility Thinkers start not with an "if" but with a "how." Here's how their thinking works:

Not *"if"* but *how* can we afford it?

Not *"if"* but *how* can we cut back current expenses?

Not *"if"* but *how* can we slash costs and cash in on this unexpected opportunity?

Not *"if"* but *how* can we clear the way to move into this area?

Not *"if"* but *how* can we get back into the marketplace again?

Not *"if"* but *how* can we make a breakthrough to find a cure?

Possibility Thinkers Are OW! Thinkers

"There is no gain without pain." Possibility Thinkers remember that. So they expect pain.

Everything that's nice has it's price. They know this.

They anticipate anguish, "but turn their scars into stars."

So they're not silly romantics, these Possibility Thinkers. They're not childish Pollyannas. They're creative realists!

Possibility Thinkers are mountain climbers. No softies last here.

Wanted: Persons with a high tolerance for pressure and pain. *Reward:* Excitement. Pride of achievement. Fulfillment at life's end! Applications *now* being accepted!

Possibility Thinkers Are VOW! Thinkers

Successful Possibility Thinkers are not afraid of commitment. However, they are not reckless in their resolve. They have asked the right questions. They have not neglected research. They have made or caused to have made studies to evaluate the possibilities. They are humble enough to pull back before the plunge if other reasonable, responsible, risk takers wisely point out pitfalls that they had not noticed before. But they are poised and prepared to make the commitment. They know that dreams will never come true by dreaming. A possibility must move from the *nesting* phase through the *testing* phase and into the *investing* phase to reach the *cresting* phase.

When God says, "Go!" the dreamer leaps. He holds nothing back. He gives his dream everything he has—and more! Total commitment! Nothing less will do.

- It's a *commitment* to a *commencement*
    —he'll get started!
- It's a *commitment* to *continuity*
    —he'll follow through!
- It's a *commitment* to *concentration*
    —he'll focus his all!
- It's a *commitment* to *completion*
    —he'll finish what he started with excellence!

The Possibility Thinker's cautious, quiet, private, secret love affair with his exciting speculation moves out of the closet into the daring daylight of a public decision! He marries the dream! Only when he recites his vows before witnesses will some people take him seriously and lend their support.

Incredible breakthroughs happen once the dreamer commits and takes the plunge. People start talking:

"He's going for it!"

"He just might make it!"

"After all—he's no flake."

"I'll lay my bets he's going to pull it off!"

"I'll bet he knows something we don't!"

So goes the positive gossip. Is it any wonder that the

dreamers attract the attention of smart people? Successful people? So don't be surprised when you hear that power people link up with them! The Vow Power is at work!

Possibility Thinkers Are POW! Thinkers

They knock problems out. As Jackie Gleason used to say, "Pow, right in the kisser!" Possibility Thinkers become winners, champions.

You're proud if you know them. You'll be humble when you become one! Humble? Yes. Not proud? Oh sure! Because humility is not the opposite of pride. It's simply the awareness that you owe a lot of people and the good Lord everything for the success that gives you so much pride today!

So . . . come back home! Begin again!

Where do you go from "out"? Back "in" to living again, that's where.

Where do you go from "out"? Anywhere you want to, that's where!

A positive thinking French woman lived in a small house in the Louisiana Bayou country. She loved it. However, she was surrounded by negative-thinking neighbor ladies who grumbled and complained about "living way *out* there in the lonely, desolate back country."

One day the positive thinker felt she had heard enough. She scolded the disagreeable and disgruntled French settlers, saying, "You live on the bayou. The bayou connects to the stream. The stream connects to the river. The river flows to the gulf. The gulf flows into the ocean. And the ocean touches the shores of the countries of the world. You all have a boat. You can go anywhere from where you are!"

Now, let's get to the deeper question: It's not *Where* but *When* do you go on from OUT?

So start exercising and practicing Possibility Thinking— the way athletes run through their regular bodybuilding stretches, the way the musician goes over and over the notes, the way the actress rehearses her lines.

I was so impressed the Sunday Milton Berle was my guest on our television program. "Make the people laugh, Milton," I told him. "You will be used by God to minister with healing humor to stress-filled and grief-stricken souls!"

Well, he took me seriously and leaned forward in his chair till his eyes were three feet from mine. He touched his ten fingertips together thoughtfully, as if in prayer. His open eyes were twinkling with inner pleasure. "Okay, Reverend Bob, here's how we can play it together."

He proceeded to outline, in detail, what he would say, and how I should react. He told me what his lines would be and offered me a witty comeback. It was marvelous. Never had I met a professional who was so well rehearsed, so thoroughly prepared, so beautifully *exact*! He took this short interview with me and my audience as seriously as if it were to be presented before the Royal Family.

With equal fervor and matching passion we must exercise, practice, rehearse our thought processes. Think "Begin!" Don't let your *possibilities* be suffocated by procrastination. Go! Now!

You want to wait till the "hurt" is all gone?

You want to wait until you have answers to every question?

You want to wait until you're sure you won't be "hurt" again and put "out" again next time the way you were last time?

You'll start when you can be sure you'll never fail?

You'll take the first step only when you can be sure you can complete the journey?

You'll make the first move when you've got the burst of inspiration?

Come on! Grow up! Enough mourning and moaning is enough!

How do you suppose I got this book written? Did I have the whole thing in my head? No. I signed a contract to deliver a book, even though I had very skimpy and scanty sketches! The publisher knew what to do to get me going. "Get Schuller to sign a contract and tie down a delivery date to lock him in!"

As the deadline drew closer I blocked out five weeks to gather my collected notes, ideas, scraps of unpublished insights and impressions and *got to work*. Did I wait until I had a mysterious, mystical, romantic burst of inspiration? Hardly. Each day in my writing studio I went to work, and if nothing came and my mind drew a blank, guess what? I picked up a fresh, clean, blank page of paper and a pen, and I simply started writing! Its amazing how it worked!

The job got done for one simple reason: I drove myself to commence! Starting is half the battle!

You'll start moving from "out" to back "in" when you start to dream again. You still have so much to offer!

Why Quit When Things Are Going to Change for the Better?

CHAPTER 8

Every End Is a New Beginning!

One day a wild and wanton wind invaded, without invitation, a peaceful nest where a family of innocent seeds lived. This wicked breeze kidnapped one defenseless little kernel and carried it away, until tired and bored with the whole adventure, it flung the helpless thing away.

And so the single seed fell onto a strange and alien shore. Here, alone and lost, it rolled across a concrete sidewalk until it was stopped by a dry crack in the barren cement. Now, an innocent, unknowing, unfriendly heel of a leather boot stepped on that seed, wedging it deep in the crevice. It was trapped. An imprisoned refugee. Discarded. Separated from family. Alone. An orphan seed clamped tightly in a deep, dark canyon. Helpless. Hopeless.

Then it happened. Deep within the heart of that seed there stirred a strange, mystic, miraculous life force that challenged death, the sidewalk, and the whole world! The heart of the captured kernel cried out, "I shall live and not die!"

When the first gentle drop of morning mist oozed into

that crack in the cement this small seed welcomed and absorbed the friendly moisture. Little wisps of dust, moved by a gentle breeze, slipped into the crack to blanket the struggling seed, which cried out once more, "I shall take root and grow!"

Softly, silently it sent out microscopic hairy roots that discovered hidden tributaries in this unlikely environment. There in miniature hidden caves the tender tendrils found more moisture, more powdery nourishment, until this wayfaring seed, swollen with determination, broke wide open and burst forth with new life. And on a bright sunny morning a little blade of grass popped out of the crack of my sidewalk, smiled at the sun, laughed at the rain, waved at the wind, and proudly declared, "Here I am, world! I made it against impossible odds! And you can too!"

If this little seed could make it, don't you think you can too? Like that seed you may have been dumped in a barren wasteland. Do you feel as though you've reached the end of the line? Are you at the end of your rope? Maybe you're severely depressed and have lost all hope—you've tried and tried only to fail again and again. Your life seems finished, your dreams washed up. Your future looms before you as a dismal enemy rather than as a potential friend.

The good news I have for you is this:
EVERY END IS A NEW BEGINNING!

What may feel like an end, may be just the darkness before the dawning of a new dream, a new challenge, a new opportunity, a new tomorrow. You have within you the power to turn terminations into transitions. You can break through this phase to a new plane. As the seed broke through the concrete to raise its head to the bright, new world, so you can break through to a new and wonderful life!

Starting Over Again—It Can Be Fun And It Can Be Done!

Nothing can appear as frustrating and overwhelming as having to start over again. All that work down the drain!

What a waste! What a tremendous loss in terms of time and energy and even finances!

Right?

WRONG!

The construction of the Panama Canal will always be an inspiration to those of us facing challenges. If it were not for the leadership of Major General George Goethals and his willingness to start over again, it is possible that the canal project would have been abandoned and doomed to utter failure! Consider, for instance, the following incident:

One section of the canal proved to be extremely difficult to dig out. It took months of arduous work to excavate and build this one section, only to have it collapse. Imagine how disheartening that would be—surely good enough cause to quit, pack up your bags, and go home!

An aide shook his head in disbelief as he and the General stood and surveyed the damage. "What do we do now, General?" he asked.

"Dig it out again!" was his answer.

Dig it out they did. And today the world enjoys the benefits of this remarkable waterway.

It may not be easy to start over again. In fact, it may be the single most difficult time in your life. But NEVER think that your efforts have been in vain or have been wasteful! You can learn from the experience, and *nothing* is more valuable than education!

In Scripture we learn how one afternoon, as Jesus spoke from the shore of Lake Gennasaret, great crowds pressed in on Him to hear His message. He noticed Peter and another fisherman washing their nets nearby. Stepping into an empty boat, Jesus asked Peter to push out into the water so He could address the crowds. When He had finished speaking, Jesus turned to Peter and said, "Now go out where it is deeper, cast your nets, and catch some fish."

"Master," Peter replied, "we have toiled all night and caught nothing" (Luke 5:5).

For Peter, a most competent fisherman, to fish all night and catch nothing is like Beverly Sills not hitting a high note. It's Arnold Palmer not shooting par. It's Norman Vincent

Peale, that great positive thinker, saying, "I can't do it! It won't work!"

Peter had toiled all night with no results whatsoever. And then Jesus recommended that he start over again!?

When you've toiled all night and caught nothing, what do you do? You use Possibility Thinking. *Never, never cash in, but cast in on the other side.*

When Peter heard Jesus' next words, he was incredulous. "Launch out into the deep and let down your nets for a catch." No doubt Peter was tired and Jesus' advice seemed preposterous, but Peter did as he was told. Suddenly, he felt the glorious weight of fish in his net, so many fish that the net began to tear as he struggled to lift it into the boat.

When you are faced with having to start over again, it is tempting to become cynical. Perhaps you want to quit school because you don't know where it is leading you. Maybe you want to give up writing because all you ever get are rejection slips. You may want to withdraw from relationships because people have treated you shabbily. Perhaps you have even tried to find assurance and joy in religion, but it, too, has come up like an empty net.

If you are tempted to look at life in terms of cynicism and futility, my friend, I want to show you how Possibility Thinking can help you find love and joy! Here's how to find self-fulfillment: First, look out for your worst enemy—yourself. Second, listen to advice from positive thinking people. Third, lower your net again. Try, and keep trying, until you make your catch.

There Are Other Fish in the Sea!

Look out for negative thinking that makes you say, "I will never find love, happiness, or success in life." Like Peter, you may be tempted to say, "The lake is empty. It is impossible to believe there are more fish."

The truth is there are other fish in the sea, and there are more tomorrows for you. No one knows for certain exactly how many fish we may catch or how many tomorrows we have, but every tomorrow is a new invitation to beautiful possibilities!

If you have lost a loved one, remember this: There are countless people in this world who are in the same boat as you. They, too, are lonely and seeking companionship. The surest cure for loneliness is to seek out others who are lonelier than you.

If you have lost a job, remember this: There are other jobs out there, maybe better than the one you lost!

In the March 23, 1987, issue of *U.S. News and World Report,* the cover story was, "You're Fired! Starting Over: A Survival Guide." The article said, "In the last five years, American corporations have eliminated the jobs of almost half a million mid- and upper-level managers with three or more years of experience. By 1990, it is estimated that an additional 400,000 of them will be laid off, too."

The statistics appear at first glance frightening, threatening. However, the article continues, "Yet in many instances the pain gives way to happy endings. Statistics are inconclusive, but the ones available indicate that many laid-off managers land jobs paying more than their former ones. They find more job satisfaction, too, usually working for smaller businesses but with a greater role in decision making. And, after starting over, they seem to enjoy greater flexibility in balancing work with family life."

The fact is that on the average at least 70 percent of all laid-off professionals were able to find new jobs! Now that's good news! That's very encouraging! The other 30 percent? Studies show many refused "smaller jobs," which, if they had taken them, could have led to something bigger and better!

So Don't Cash In—Cast In!

Throw out a line. You can't catch fish if you don't put a baited hook in the water.

In 1948 an engineer named Theodore Elliot solved a problem that had hindered commerce for decades. For years farmers and businessmen had wished for a railroad that would cross from New York to Canada. But to build such a railroad, a bridge was needed to span the Niagara River. Traditional bridge building schemes simply would not work. But Mr. Elliot conceived a brilliant solution—the first suspension bridge. He envisioned supportive towers twenty-four by eighty feet high on either side of the roaring, raging waters of the Niagara River. From the towers he would suspend a cable which in turn would support the bridge.

But he had one problem. How could he get started? There was no way to work from a boat at that point on the river. There was no shoreline to work from either, only sheer, rocky cliffs. And he knew that *beginning was half done.*

So he decided to start by stringing a cable from one side of the river to the other. "A cable made from 36 strands of #10 wire will be thick and sturdy enough to suspend two buckets capable of holding two workers. These workers could go from side to side and begin construction of the bridge," he said.

"But how can you get a steel cable that thick across the gorge?" someone asked. "You can't throw it across. It's too heavy."

Elliot was puzzled for a moment. Then he got an idea: Why not have a contest for the kids in the neighborhood—a kite flying contest? Elliot announced the contest and offered a prize of ten dollars to the first boy who could fly a kite across the gorge and tie the rope down on the other side. There were many contestants, for ten dollars was a lot of money for a lad in those days. But none succeeded until one day an eleven-year-old boy named Homer Walsh took advantage of a good south wind. His kite took off, and instead of falling short as all the others had, it landed on the other side. His friend, who was waiting across the river, tied the string down on the other side. Homer collected the prize!

The next day Elliot tied the kite string to a slightly heavier rope. He pulled the rope across the gorge so that it spanned the gap. Then he tied that rope to a still thicker rope and pulled it across. This rope he attached to the steel cable.

By repeating the process, he strung the cable from one side of the gorge to the other, thus enabling the two workers to go back and forth and begin the construction of the suspension bridge.

CAST IN! Throw out a line! Take the first step! Be willing to start small! It beats sitting at home, watching daytime television. You simply must make a positive move!

Look at What You Have Left—Never Look at What You Have Lost!

Be of good cheer! You still have what matters most: 1) freedom to move in many directions; 2) freedom to choose how you will react to what has happened to you; 3) freedom to choose to let this turn you into a bitter or a better human being; 4) freedom to make a breakthrough for yourself.

There still are:

- Countless new possibilities!
- Overlooked and underrated fantastic opportunities!
- Talents that you have been neglecting!
- Assets that have been lying dormant!
- Open doors waiting to swing out!

What an exciting prospect! And you have the freedom and the power within you to identify which direction your life should take.

There's Hope for a Breakthrough for You!

If you are at the bottom, weighed down by overwhelming circumstances, if you are at the edge of panic, the most dangerous thing you can do is to make a negative, irreversible decision.

Keep believing, and there will be a breakthrough. You *will* break through the challenges that you are currently facing. You *will* break through the defeats that have set you back. You *will* emerge on the other side and say, *"It was all for the better!"*

The first question you will probably ask is: *When will a*

breakthrough happen? It could happen today, tomorrow, or the next day. I don't know when, and neither can you. God alone knows the answer to that question.

The next question you may ask is: *How long can I hold on?* A lot longer than you think you can!

Every psychiatrist will say it: "We see patients, month after month, year after year. Suddenly one day, through nothing specific that we could tell that we did, the skin that drooped and was gray becomes pink; the eye that was dull as if asleep gets a sparkle! It's a phenomenal moment. For hope is a phenomenon! We don't know what triggers the birth of hope or where it comes from. We don't think it comes from us. What we do know is what happens in the person! When a person finds hope, there is total renewal."

You can find new hope when you realize that today is the BEGINNING! *What looks like an end never is unless you decide to make it the end.*

God isn't finished with you yet. Just give Him a chance to break through. There is a breakthrough for you. But remember, the breakthrough is up to YOU! It probably will not happen until you go beyond the limits you have accepted for your life.

Going Beyond the Limits!

We all have self-imposed limitations that hold us back. If we have failed to realize success or if our success is limited, it is probably due to preconceptions that are throwing an invisible barrier across our paths. The puzzle below illustrates how we can be held back from breaking through. The challenge is to connect all nine dots with four straight lines, *without lifting your pencil from the paper.*

It seems impossible to intersect all nine dots with four straight lines. But how do you move something from the impossible to the possible? Answer: *Go beyond the limits.* When you go beyond the limits, the impossible becomes possible. When you go beyond the limits, you will be able to intersect all nine dots with four straight lines. (Turn to page 208 to see the solution.)

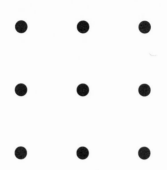

Break through your self-imposed limitations. "I can't find a single job in this whole town." Well, why limit yourself to this town? This state? Get up and move to where the jobs are. "I can only do carpentry. And they're not hiring carpenters these days." Why limit yourself to one trade? Use your free time to learn new skills! No one said when you drew four straight lines that they couldn't go beyond the extent of the dots. *That was a limitation you imposed upon yourself.* And when you impose these limitations, the puzzle becomes unsolvable. You can break away from the self-imposed limits of the dots when you *think bigger*!

Are you having financial difficulties? Probably you've imposed a mental limitation on your earning power.

Recently I had breakfast with one of my church members. A man came in with a briefcase, leading another person behind him. They sat down in the booth next to mine.

The person who had been led said to the man with the valise, "Well, I'd sure like the job."

The man said, "How much do you want to earn?"

The hopeful employee replied, "All I need to earn is four hundred a week." I thought, *isn't that sad.* Sad because he is setting his own limits. So he may never earn more.

Don't wall yourself in by refusing to stretch the boundaries *you* have set up!

Does this seem and sound impossible to you today? It will probably require some tough faith. Faith is leaping over the fence! It's crossing the mountains. It's going beyond the boundaries. It's breaking through the limitations that you and others have set! It is seeing beyond the end to a bright new beginning and a beautiful new tomorrow.

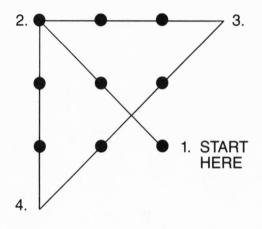

Don't Throw a Curtain Across Tomorrow!

Hazel Wright was a well-known philanthropist. She gave large gifts to many worthy causes in her lifetime, including $1 million to buy and install the pipe organ in the Crystal Cathedral. Today it is called the finest pipe organ in any church in the world. It carries her name: The Hazel Wright Organ.

Hazel always loved music and she always loved to dance. Once, when she was healthy and well, she asked me to dance. I had to say to her, "Hazel, I never learned to dance. I wouldn't know how to dance if I wanted to."

Later Hazel became very sick. Her illness was diagnosed as a malignancy! With the progression of her disease, she went into what was, according to the doctors, a death coma. Members of our church prayed for her. I prayed for her. I would stand by her bed and talk to her as if she could understand. Then I saw a faint smile, and I knew that within her soul she was getting the message.

Then it happened! It was amazing! The doctors were surprised! Hazel awoke from her death coma. They sent her home from the hospital, even though she was still a very sick woman and, from a medical standpoint, her prognosis was not good.

I called on her days before she died. She was extremely tired. There was no sparkle in her eye. I picked up her thin, bony hands, held them above the sheets, looked at her and said, "Hazel, I know there's one thing you've always wanted to do in your life, and that's dance with Dr. Schuller. Hazel, let's dance."

Holding her hands, I swayed them back and forth and hummed the tune to the song, "Shall we dance?" Her face just beamed. Her skin became pink. The eyes sparkled and looked as dashing as they must have been when she was eighteen years old.

I said, "Hazel, what can I give you? Is there any other gift that you would like?"

She said, "Yes! I know what I'd like. I'd like a calendar for the new year, a big one, with room to write lots of things in."

That's HOPE! As long as you can breathe, you should have a calendar—a big one with room to write lots of things. There is no such thing as an end in the road; there are always bends in the road. And no matter how wide the barrier may seem to be, you can always break through it if you can hope and if you can look forward to a new tomorrow!

Tomorrow Is Today!

The exciting thing to realize is that tomorrow is a lot closer than you realize. In fact, for many of you it is already here! And as contradictory as it may sound, "Tomorrow is TODAY!"

A few years ago when I was visiting the Holy Land and staying at a hotel by the Sea of Galilee, I picked up the phone and called Arvella, who was back in California. It was 5 A.M., Tuesday, in Galilee, and 7 P.M., Monday, in California.

My wife and I chatted briefly. I shared my experiences with her. And then instead of saying goodbye, Arvella said, "Have a wonderful tomorrow."

I said, "But tomorrow is already here." And in fact, that's what it was. My today was her tomorrow.

Tomorrow is today! Don't worry about tomorrow. Concentrate on today, for your tomorrow is today. How you think and how you act today will determine your future. To an overwhelming degree, you can control your life, your changes, by how you perceive them. So plan and pray your way toward tomorrow.

Today Is a New Day!

The sun is shining, the sky is blue!
There's a new day dawning for me and you.
With every dawning of the sun
New possibilities have just begun.
With every breaking of the morn
Fresh opportunities are newly born.

Do you know what will happen tomorrow? Guess!
• Cures will be found.
• New inventions will be created.
• Miracle drugs will come on the market.
• Oppressive laws will be repelled.
• Secrets of conflict resolution will be discovered.
• New businesses will be organized.
• New careers will be launched.

Get ready for tomorrow because YOU will have a part to play in it!

*Whatever
You Do Today*

*Do It
Better Tomorrow.*

CHAPTER 9

Say, "Farewell to Failure!"

Say, "Hello to Success!"

You are ready now to say "farewell to failure" and "hello to success."

What is the magic ingredient that can insure success and eliminate failure from our lives? It is FAITH! Possibility Thinking is just another word for faith.

You will be controlled by either positive thoughts or negative thoughts. One of two emotions will dominate and drive you: either fear or faith. If you are not living by faith, then you will automatically be living by fear. Never surrender the leadership of your life to fear!

Of course, a capacity for fear is part of our survival instinct. But compulsive fear is something else. This is a vague, ever-present sense of foreboding, mixed with anxiety and worry. Compulsive fear is not normal in that it does not come from God. Much of it comes from the unbelieving minds of negative thinkers.

Dr. E. Stanley Jones, one of the most learned minds of this century, summed it up beautifully:

I see that I am inwardly fashioned for faith and not for fear. Fear is not my native land; faith is. I am so made that worry and anxiety are sand in the machinery of life: faith is oil. I live better by faith and confidence than by fear and doubt and anxiety. In anxiety and worry my being is gasping for breath—these are not my native air. But in faith and confidence I breathe freely—these are my native air. A Johns Hopkins doctor says that "We do not know why it is that worriers die sooner than the non-worriers, but that is a fact." But I, who am simple of mind, think I know: we are inwardly constructed, in nerve and tissue, and brain cell and soul, for faith and not for fear. God made us that way. To live by worry is to live against reality.[1]

No force, no emotion is more paralyzing than fear. It stops a salesperson about to make a call; the young man about to propose marriage; a job hunter about to seek an interview; an executive moments before making a decisive move; a seeker after truth about to commit his life to God.

In the whole sordid, sorry spectacle of human fears, none is more destructive and defeating than the fear of failure. Reject fear as the controlling force of your life. Discard such negative thinking as *flawed thinking!*

Some of you have lived your whole lives in fear. You have been taught to be skeptical and suspicious. You believe it is prudent to be cautious. In the process you may actually have become addicted to a deeply rooted, pessimistic mental outlook.

You may be caught in a web of anxiety like the poor widow who lived in the Orient. She had two sons and depended entirely on their meager little business. Every day she worried about their business, fretting and hoping that they would do well.

One son sold umbrellas. So when the mother awakened in the morning she would look to see if the sun was shining

---

[1]E. Stanley Jones, *Abundant Living* (Nashville: Abingdon, 1976).

or if it looked like rain. If it was dark and cloudy she would gleefully say, "Oh, he will surely sell umbrellas today."

If the sun was shining, she would be miserable all day because she feared that nobody would buy her son's umbrellas.

The widow's other son sold fans. Every morning when the poor old widow looked to the skies, if the sun was hidden and it looked like a rainy day, she would get very depressed and moan, "Nobody's going to buy my son's fans today."

No matter what the weather was, this poor old lady had something to fret about. With such an attitude she was bound to lose.

One day she ran into a friend who said, "You've got it all wrong, my dear. The truth is that you can't help but win. You live off both of your sons. If the sun is shining, people will buy fans; if it rains, they'll buy umbrellas. Either way—sun or rain—you win!"

From then on, according to the parable, she was a happy and peaceful woman!

The process of success will require the mental discipline on your part to reject flawed thinking. This will not be easy, for you have probably worked all your life on creating and polishing an elaborate, intricate system of negative thinking. To "convert"—to "change" to become a mentally "born again" person—means discarding and walking away from the person you have been. You may even feel you are walking away from a lifetime of invested work!

I shall never forget the trip I took with my wife up the Nile River to the Aswan Dam. There we saw the site from which the famous Egyptian obelisks were cut and polished. The world-renowned sculptured pieces were all mined from this one granite quarry. And each obelisk was carved by the Egyptians from one chunk of granite.

These monuments unfortunately have been dispersed throughout the world. One was brought to London. Another stands in St. Peter's Square. I've also seen one in Paris and another in Istanbul. There are still a few left in Egypt, but the biggest one of all still lies in the quarry.

The Egyptians spent decades cutting it out, chiseling it, filing it, sanding it, but there it lies. It is 14 feet square at the base and 142 feet long. I walked all over it. It's just lying there. Why? Because just before they got ready to move it, the experts looked at it, and they saw what no one else could see—flaws in the granite. And because of those flaws, they chose to abandon it.

If you are living by fear, then see this as a flaw, for negative thinking is flawed thinking. It will not stand up! It will crack for sure! Walk away from negative thinking. Dare to live by faith!

You may have lived your entire life with skepticism, cynicism, agnosticism, and pure secularism. You need to realize that there's a flaw in this kind of thinking.

I'm asking you today—if you've lived without belief in God and Jesus, if you're a skeptic and cynic, and an unbeliever and a doubter—to examine your way of thinking. You were designed to be a believer!

If you want to say "farewell to failure," get rid of your fears. Fears rest on silent assumptions that distort thinking. For instance—consider the fear of failure. It carries the silent assumptions that if I fail, I'll be embarrassed, I may be laughed at, I'll be ashamed. Enter Possibility Thinking therapy: Why do you cringe at embarrassment? Will it kill you? Actually, you are assuming that if you're laughed at, you will lose your self-respect; you will no longer be able to love yourself, and you'll lose your self-esteem!

The Possibility Thinking counselor can expose the distortion in thinking caused by negative, silent assumptions. Faith is injected to replace fear and further clarify the distorted, unhealthy thinking: "Just think—you might fail, but you'll be so proud that you really tried! And good people will respect you for your courage and adventuresome spirit!

So fear thinking must be replaced by faith thinking.

The Bible is filled with commands to be courageous. Someone counted the "fear nots" in the Bible and discovered that there are 365 verses with this divine command—one for every day of the year! Verses such as:

- *"Fear not. . . . When you pass through the waters . . . they shall not overflow you. When you walk through the fire, you shall not be burned. . . . For I am the LORD your God. I will be with you"* (Isa. 43:1–3).
- *"Be strong and of good courage; do not be afraid, nor be dismayed, for the LORD your God is with you wherever you go"* (Josh. 1:9).
- *"For God has not given us a spirit of fear, but of power and of love and of a sound mind"* (2 Tim. 1:7).
- *"If you have faith as a mustard seed you will say to this mountain, 'Move from here to there,' and it will move; and nothing will be impossible for you"* (Matt. 17:20).

You can help wipe out failure-producing fears from your life through Possibility Thinking—or Dynamic Faith. Observe now how *faith is the force that sets you free to succeed.*

Look at the following chart (page 221). It illustrates how faith works in your life to free you from negative emotions and release the powerful, positive emotions that totally transform your entire being!

Check the chart carefully to see how and why faith is such a matchless superpower to completely turn negative lives into positive lives. Faith sets you free from downgrading, degrading, negative emotions and replaces them with success-generating emotions!

Start by reading down column one. See how FAITH leads to *dreaming.* Dreaming leads to *desiring.* Desiring leads to *praying.* Praying leads to *beginning.* Beginning leads to *deciding.* Deciding leads to *planning.* Planning leads to *waiting.* Waiting leads to *paying the price.* Paying the price leads to *managing problems,* which leads to *expecting success!* This process spells "Faith in Depth!"

Now read down the second column. Faith produces a FORCE called *purpose,* which produces a force called *passion,* which produces a force called *hope,* which produces a force called *commitment*. Commitment produces a force called *direction*, which leads to a force called *thinking-through*, which generates a force called *patience*. Patience produces a force called *determination*, which produces a force called *control*, which releases a force called *enthusiasm!*

Now read down the third column.

Yes, faith is dreaming, which releases a powerful purpose, which sets you FREE from the *blahs*. When you are free of the blahs, you are free from *boredom*. When you are free from boredom, you are free from *anxiety*. When you are free from anxiety, then you are free from *inertia*. When you are free from inertia, you are free from *indecision*. When you are free from indecision, you are free from *confusion*. When you are free from confusion, then you are free from *impatience*. When you are free from impatience, then you are free from *expediency*. When you are free from expediency, then you are free from *defeatism*. When you are free from defeatism, then you are free from the *fear of failure*.

Faith frees you from negative emotions that hold you back because it replaces them with positive forces that propel you onward and upward. Read down the last column to see where faith leads. First you get interested! Then Excited! Encouraged! Involved! Dedicated! Organized! Consistent! Reliable! Optimistic! Successful!

Now, read each line across horizontally! See how:

FAITH is the FORCE that sets you FREE to SUCCEED.

The next line illustrates the process of success.

Dreaming → Purpose → Blahs → Interested

Dreaming produces a force called purpose which releases you from failure-producing blahs and gets you interested in really succeeding.

The next line illustrates the amazing process of success.

Desiring → *Passion* → *Boredom* → *Excited*

Dreaming becomes desiring which generates a force stronger than mere purpose—passion! Passion frees you from boredom and instead of merely being interested, you are now genuinely excited!

The next line illustrates the growing and developing process of success.

Praying → *Hope* → *Anxiety* → *Encouraged*

Desiring gives way to praying, which produces hope, which frees you from anxiety, which gives you real encouragement.

See how your success is evolving—the process of success is working for you like a seed becoming a plant becoming a bud becoming a flower!

Read the next line. Faith moves from the praying stage to the beginning stage.

Beginning → *Commitment* → *Inertia* → *Involved*

Encouraged, you now get started. This releases a force called commitment! Commitment frees you from inertia! You are now involved. This sets you up for the next stage of success.

Read the next line, and you'll see the evolution clearly!

Deciding → *Direction* → *Indecision* → *Dedicated*

Now faith becomes deciding—you've made a decision. This releases a force called direction which frees you from indecision and leaves you solidly dedicated.

Wow! Now look what happens!

Planning → *Thinking-Through* → *Confusion* → *Organized*

Faith enters the planning stage and generates a force called thinking-through which helps you to "sort it all out" and free your mind from confusion. Now, you feel organized! Fantastic progress is being made in this process called success!

Your faith now will be ready for the "testing" phase.

Waiting → *Patience* → *Impatience* → *Consistent*

You'll encounter difficulties. Your success may stumble and falter. So your faith now becomes a "waiting game." A fantastic force called patience frees you from dangerous and potentially fatal impatience and leaves you with consistency or stability.

Where does this road lead! Read the next horizontal line.

Paying the Price → *Determination* → *Expediency* → *Reliable*

Paying the price—that's the force of faith at this stage in the success process. Invest heavily and you release an incredible force called determination. Instantly you are free from the temptation to take a cheap and swift exit called expediency. Upshot?! You stick it out. You don't quit. You are reliable!

Now your faith is expressed in managing problems (rather than in running from them).

Managing Problems → *Control* → *Defeatism* → *Optimistic*

Managing problems generates a powerful force called control which frees you from being defeated by your difficulties so that you emerge optimistic!

You're ready for the last line.

FAITH is the	FORCE that sets you	FREE	TO be	SUCCEED
		From		
Dreaming	Purpose	Blahs		Interested
Desiring	Passion	Boredom		Excited
Praying	Hope	Anxiety		Encouraged
Beginning	Commitment	Inertia		Involved
Deciding	Direction	Indecision		Dedicated
Planning	Thinking-Through	Confusion		Organized
Waiting	Patience	Impatience		Consistent
Paying the price	Determination	Expediency		Reliable
Managing Problems	Control	Defeatism		Optimistic
Expecting Success	Enthusiasm	Failure		Successful

Expecting Success → Enthusiasm → Failure → Successful

Faith now is a matter of expecting success. This produces the ultimate force called enthusiasm. You are now set free from failure and you will emerge successful. Now you can see how *Faith* is the *Force* that sets you free! Now you can see that the process of success is the *living* out, from one level to another to another, of a positive faith!

CHAPTER 10

Now

Come Alive

With HOPE!

I made two trips to Minneapolis, Minnesota, to be with my friend Hubert H. Humphrey after he became ill with cancer. Hubert had just been told he had only a few months to live, and his family had invited me to come and try to help motivate him to make one last trip back to Washington. All his life he had been a fighter, but for the first time he was defeated. Hope had left him. Despair had moved in.

"Hubert," I asked, "how did you manage to come back after your defeats?" He had experienced his share—most notably his defeat by Richard Nixon for president.

"Get my little notebook, Muriel," Hubert called to his wife. She handed him a small, black book. It was stuffed with clippings that hung out like ladies' slips below their skirts. Heavy rubber bands were wrapped around the middle of the bulging book. Carefully with his thin and weak hands Hubert removed the rubber bands and began to share inspiring notes collected in a lifetime: uplifting ideas, positive aphorisms, inspiring quotations. "Oh, here's the Bible verse you sent me, Bob, when I was in New York's Kettering Clinic," he said. "My staff brought in a six-inch file of telegrams. Yours was on the top! Above President Carter, no less! Here it is! 'Dear Hubert. Hang in there. Never give up till God calls you. "For I know the thoughts that I think toward you, says the LORD, thoughts of peace and not of evil, to give you a future and a hope" (Jer. 29:11).' That's great! That's a tremendous Bible verse, Bob!"

Now I saw hope rise. He came alive again. And before I knew it he said, "Muriel, I think we ought to go back to Washington, once more!"

The next day President Jimmy Carter in Air Force One stopped at Minneapolis and took Hubert Humphrey back to Washington, to the greatest days of honor and glory ever heaped on a living American. So Hubert's success was unending. And his failures were never final!

A few months later Hubert slipped away quietly. The call came to my sunny California office inviting me to deliver the funeral sermon in Minneapolis. In zero-degree weather we came from all over America for his funeral. Billy Graham. Jesse Jackson. President Jimmy Carter. The leading senators from both sides of the political fence. Hollywood celebrities. All three networks were standing by to air the service live to tens of millions around America. Now it was time for my message. It was for me then and remains today my greatest honor. My words offered to HHH are words I offer as a grand possibility for your life, yes, and for mine, too: "He comes to the end of this life with Pride behind him, Love around him, and Hope ahead of him."

A news reporter said later, "Hubert Humphrey finally lost the battle to cancer." The cynic could charge: "He kept on hoping to the end, but it was a false hope." Really? The truth is each day he lived in hope was an alive day!

Possibility Thinking has been faulted by more than one cynic and critic for generating false hope. Wait a minute! Hope, whether it is fulfilled or not, is never a vain and false promise. It immediately and instantaneously rewards the hopeful person with rescue from despair!

All we can be sure of is the present moment. So hope is

its own immediate reward. Morbid depression is replaced with a bright and cheerful outlook! Yesterday is past. Tomorrow may never come. If I can take today and put sunshine and sparkle into it, have I not blessed a life? No hope is ever false if it rescues a discouraged heart from despair for one uplifting minute.

"But when Hubert Humphrey died, his success finally ended, didn't it?" I think not, but your answer depends on whether you have a positive or a negative perspective on life and death. Did he die or is it more accurate to say he was born again into eternal life? Does the unborn infant die when it leaves the womb? Tell the about-to-be-born child that he is going to enter a world of color, sounds, and people. If the unborn infant could communicate, it would ask questions you and I could never answer: "What are colors? What is sound? What are people?" We could only send this message: "Have faith! You'll die to one world but be born into another!"

So people stand on the shore waving goodbye to those on the departing ship while others on another shore wave a welcome: "Here she comes!"

So I offer you the most challenging idea, the *ultimate possibility*—the invitation to become a Super-Possibility Thinker and follow the person who in my opinion is the greatest Possibility Thinker who ever lived—Jesus Christ.

He said it, "If you have faith as a mustard seed, you will ' say to this mountain, 'Move,' . . . and nothing will be impossible to you!" He taught that we could be saved from death to eternal life! He taught that success has no ending! That He would "be there" to forgive us of our sins and welcome us into his eternal company! Forgiveness! That's throwing out failure *once and for all!* That's heaven!

Real Salvation Is a Real Possibility!

For years, authentic, emotionally healthy Christians have expressed a natural enthusiasm and ebullient joy. They spend a great deal of time, energy, and love giving of themselves. When asked why, they would probably be quick to quote John 3:16, "For God so loved the world that He gave His only begotten Son, that whoever believes in Him should not perish but have everlasting life." They speak of being saved, of being born again, of the salvation of their souls.

What does it mean to be saved?

Well, whether you realize it or not, God has probably saved you from physical tragedies. You will never know what you have been spared by the grace of God. Occasionally we are able to catch glimpses of what we have been saved from.

I think of the time, for instance, when I went to be with Billy Graham at a crusade in Las Vegas. My reservations were at the MGM Grand Hotel. However, one of Billy's staff members picked me up at the airport and said, "If you don't mind we have changed your reservations to the Hilton. Billy wants you there because that's where he is, and it is closer to the convention center."

So that night I slept in the Hilton. The next morning I watched in horror as the MGM burned and 107 people perished. And I thank my God that He prevented me from staying in that hotel that night.

In April of 1986 I once again felt the protective, saving power of God. My wife and I were in London, en route to Africa for a conference. It was only days after the United States had bombed Libya. I had asked the church congregation to pray for our safety.

Our hotel was near the U.S. Embassy. I said to Arvella, "I need to run out and have our tickets rewritten since we didn't have time to do that in Los Angeles." So at about four in the afternoon I walked down Oxford Street to the British Airways building, which also houses the offices of American Airlines and American Express. I gave British Airways my tickets. They informed me that it would take them about forty minutes, so I sat down and read the travel brochures.

Forty-five minutes later I got my tickets. I walked out of the British Airways office at a quarter to five. At four the next morning the place blew up. Totally! You probably heard about it on the news. The experts think that the bomb had already been placed when I was sitting there. The amazing thing is that, according to the experts, the bomb was probably meant to go off at 4:00 *P.M.* instead of 4:00 *A.M.* By the grace of God, the bomb went off when the building was deserted. Nobody was killed and I'm alive!

The salvation of God is incredible. Most of us will never know what we have been saved from. But some of you know. Some of you walk minus a leg or minus an arm from an accident or disease that almost killed you—but DIDN'T! For you, it's easy to believe that *God loves you.*

God has saved us—more than we know—in more ways than we are aware of. The word "saved" appears numerous times throughout the Bible:

- "Sing to the LORD, all the earth;/Proclaim the good news of His salvation from day to day" (1 Chron. 16:23).
- "You shall call His name JESUS, for He will save His people from their sins" (Matt. 1:21).

Salvation! It's a life-transforming word. But what does it really mean to be saved? This chart will help explain:

HERE'S HOW SALVATION CAN GIVE YOU THE ULTIMATE SUCCESS!
God's Love Saves Us . . .

from Cynicism .... to Possibility Thinking!
from Blind Doubt .... to Eye-opening Faith!
from Defensive Fear .... to Receptive Love!
from Stubborn Pride .... to Honest Humility!
from Dishonest Denial .... to Frank Admission!
from Guilt .... to Pardon!
from Condemnation .... to Forgiveness!
from Aloneness .... to Togetherness
from Shame .... to Glory!
from Egotism .... to Self-esteem!
from Morbid Moodiness .... to Authentic Motivation!
from Weakness .... to Power!
from Evil .... to Holiness!
from Despair .... to Hope!

No wonder we can come alive! With hope! *If* we are *saved*!

Saved: From Cynicism to Possibility Thinking!

Cynicism is arrogance. It is the mental pattern of the elitist, who considers himself to be too intelligent and too brilliant to be taken in. He is such a perceptive critic that his immediate defensive reaction to any positive proposal is negative objection.

Salvation begins when we shift from cynicism to Possibility Thinking. This tender, cautious adjustment of an internal attitude toward a positive proposal is the first step toward salvation.

Some of you reading this book are admittedly cynics. When you hear about born-again Christians, you say to yourself, "Oh, I know all about these born-again Christians. They're not as genuine and loving as they say they are. I've met a few of them myself, and I have to say they're no different from me!"

Oh! But there is a difference! They live life on the level of faith, whereas you live life on the level of suspicion. They are quick to believe, whereas you are quick to doubt. If you are a cynic, start by admitting it to yourself, for cynicism has to give way to Possibility Thinking before the liberating process of salvation can begin.

Saved: From Blind Doubt to Eye-opening Faith!

The cynic would say, "The Christian has blind *faith*," assuming that a cynic's doubts give instead an eye-opening *understanding*. Not true!

- *Doubt* BLINDS you to all kinds of possibilities!
- *Faith* OPENS your eyes to all kinds of opportunities!

Saved: From Defensive Fear to Receptive Love!

The nonbeliever tends to be cynical, living by blind doubt and defensiveness. He is afraid of conversion. He is afraid of being born again. He is afraid of religion. He is afraid of emotion.

You have to be saved from *defensive fear* to *receptive*

It's
Easier for God
to Say,
"No!" to Us

Than for Him
to Get
Us to Say,
"Yes!" to Him!

love. When you dare to make that move, you may be surprised to find tears in your eyes. It takes courage to be receptive to love.

Saved: From Stubborn Pride to Honest Humility!

The person who is saved from stubborn pride is able to say with honest humility:
- "There's a lot I really don't know. Can you fill me in?"
- "I thought I had all the answers, but now I'm not sure they are accurate."
- "My professor in college was a die-hard atheist. I thought he was so smart. Now I'm not sure."

Humility is honesty. It is the sure way to learn the truth. On the other hand, stubborn pride can perpetuate inaccuracies and fallacies.

Saved: From Dishonest Denial to Frank Admission!

Once you are saved from stubborn pride to honest humility, you can be saved from dishonest denial. There is such a thing as honest denial, but we are concerned here with DIShonest denial. An example of dishonest denial is the alcoholic who denies that he has a problem with alcohol. You can be saved from dishonest denial to frank and honest admission when you can say, "I need help. I'm *not* perfect."

Frank, honest admission is what the Bible calls confession. "If we confess our sins, He is faithful and just to forgive us our sins and to cleanse us from all unrighteousness" (1 John 1:9).

Saved: From Guilt to Pardon!

Absolutely no emotional experience is more healing to the mind and soul than to be honestly pardoned, forgiven of your sins, and restored to your post and position of honor. Think of it! Every decent person hurts inside with guilt when he knows he has fallen short. Gone is all guilt when we accept the offer of Jesus Christ to be our Savior!

Saved: From Condemnation to Forgiveness!

When you are saved from guilt to pardon, you're saved from condemnation to forgiveness. The rest of your life you can know that God will not condemn you, not now, not tomorrow, not ever! Even if others disagree with you or don't understand you or are critical of you, that doesn't matter as long as you do not live under condemnation but under forgiveness.

Saved: From Aloneness to Togetherness!

No longer are you lost in isolationism; rather you are brought into what I call relationalism. You see, a person who is not saved is basically cynical. He is blinded by doubt from positive relationships. He is frozen by defensive fear, stubborn pride, and dishonest denial. He lives under guilt and subconscious condemnation. That kind of a person does not move out honestly, openly, and easily to make friends.

God's love saves you from loneliness. It frees you to make healthy, rewarding relationships with others and with God. When you are saved you are *together* with God and not *separated* from Him. It's what the Bible calls reconciliation.

Christ is called the reconciler. He reconciles us to God. That's why the word atonement in the Bible means "at-one-ment." When I am saved, when I have been atoned for, I am at one with God. So I become a part of a community of believers, saved *from* aloneness, saved *to* togetherness.

Saved: From Shame to Glory!

When I'm saved from shame to glory, I'm born again. I no longer see myself as a shameful person, but I see myself as the glorious creation that God lovingly made. I see myself as having a mind that can think God's thoughts, having a heart that can love the way Jesus loves, having hands that can help give people a lift, having lips that can convey a message of hope and courage.

The message of salvation according to the Bible is this: We are saved from shame to glory, "Christ in you, the hope of glory" (Col. 1:27).

I lectured on this point at the American Psychiatric Association's convention in Los Angeles. The psychiatrists who heard it were amazingly intrigued by this message. I mention this for one reason—nobody has a better treatment for your mind, your emotions, your soul than God does!

Saved: From Egotism to a Healthy Self-esteem!

We're saved from shame to glory and from egotism to a healthy self-esteem. Egotism is a mark of selfish persons: They want their own way. Egotists will do it their way so that they can get the credit. Their hunger for personal glory feeds their egos. Even their guilt and shame urge the ego on. People like this are confident that if their egos are fulfilled, that will cover any shame and give them glory. That's just not true. It's a false description, a dead end, empty hope.

Once you are "friends with the Lord," you have a healthy self-esteem and the ego problems are solved.

Saved: From Morbid Moodiness to Authentic Motivation!

When—
- Cynicism has been replaced with Possibility Thinking,
- Blind doubt has been replaced with eye-opening faith,
- Defensive fear has been replaced with receptive love,
- Stubborn pride has been replaced with honest humility,
- Dishonest denial has been replaced with frank and honest confession,
- Guilt has been replaced with pardon,
- Condemnation has been replaced with forgiveness,
- Aloneness has been replaced with togetherness,
- Shame has been replaced with glory,
- Egotism has been replaced with self-esteem,

then—you are emotionally set up for a big idea, a wonderful dream!

God Himself can come bursting into your life telling you what you can do and what you can accomplish. Suddenly you catch a glimpse of the contribution you can make.

Saved: From Weakness to Power!

Now you are driven by inner enthusiasm, not external pressures to persevere. Enthusiasm replaces endurance! Oddly enough, enthusiasm becomes a power to keep you keeping on! You are saved from weakness to power!

When you catch a vision of what God can do with and through your life, then you begin to believe the Bible verse, "I can do all things through Christ who strengthens me" (Phil. 4:13).

Salvation means that you can begin to think that you *can* make a contribution!

On my first trip to South Korea, in the early 1960s, there wasn't a single green tree growing. After the war the people had stripped all the green leaves off and eaten them. Then they stripped off the bark and cooked it for broth. Finally they cut down the trunks and the branches and burned the wood to keep from freezing in the minus-twenty-degree weather.

Nobody had a bicycle, much less a car! The streets were filled with people milling about on foot. You talk about being hopelessly trapped. These people were trapped, but they were trapped with HOPE!

The Koreans have made tremendous progress. They have moved from weakness to power. How did they do it? They *believed* they could do it! They became genuine Possibility Thinkers! That produced energy to fuel their drive. No country worked harder. "The Koreans are the only people who work so hard that they make the Japanese look lazy" became a standard comment from world business leaders.

Saved: From Evil to Holiness!

What is evil? And what is holiness?

- *Evil* is defusing, ignoring, and neglecting the opportunities that God sends your way. *Holiness* is becoming the person God wants you to be.
- *Evil* is self-centered, self-seeking living. *Holiness* is asking, "How can I do God's work in my lifetime?"

Sir James Young Simpson lived a "holy" life (not necessarily a perfect life but definitely a *productive* one). He gave to the world a great gift—the gift of anesthesia. If you ever doubt that the discovery was a gift, consider the excruciating pain that accompanied surgery prior to his discovery.

Sir James was born in Scotland in 1811, the eighth child of the local baker. His parents decided he should be a scholar, so he was enrolled at Edinburgh University when he was only fourteen years old. In 1830, not yet out of his teens, he became a member of the Royal College of Surgeons but could not practice because of his youth. Consequently, he became an assistant to Dr. Thomas, a professor of pathology, who encouraged him to go into obstetrics.

When young James started in obstetrics, it was considered the least of the medical arts. But he elevated the science to a noble branch of medicine.

From the very beginning, Dr. Simpson was concerned about the pain of surgery and childbirth, and he strove to find ways to ease it. When ether was used in 1847 in the United States, Dr. Simpson tried it but was unsatisfied with the inconveniences it created in labor.

Dr. Simpson and two of his assistants experimented on themselves, trying to find something that would work. On November 4, 1847, Dr. Simpson's assistants inhaled chloroform and immediately passed out. After subsequent testing, chloroform was used in a public surgical demonstration in the Royal Infirmary in Edinburgh. The ultimate seal of approval was given to the use of chloroform when Queen Victoria used it during childbirth.

Chloroform was not Simpson's only contribution to medicine. He continually worked at improving and upgrading the state of hospitals and care of the sick.

Any of us would be proud to have made the contributions and discoveries that Sir James Young Simpson made. Knighted in 1866, he was the recipient of numerous awards and honors.

Yet, when he was asked by a journalist what he considered his greatest discovery, Sir James Y. Simpson replied, "That I have a Savior!"

Saved: from despair to hope!

Salvation is being saved from despair to hope, a belief that no matter what happens—even death—I will live through it.

You ask me, "Dr. Schuller, do you believe in heaven? Do you believe in hell?"

Well I've never been to either place, so I can't speak from personal experience. The Bible gives us some rough sketches of what we can expect, but most of the details are open to individual interpretation. There is very little that I can tell you with certainty about heaven or hell.

What I CAN tell you is there is another authority who knows. And I have found that it is better to trust a genuine authority. If you want the right answers, not just any answer, then go to the right person.

Recently I was on a quick, twenty-four-hour, out-of-town trip. As I was returning through an airport, I stopped at a candy store to buy chocolates for my wife. Arvella loves chocolates! And she happens to particularly love chocolate-covered nuts. I walked into the Fannie Mae candy store where a clerk greeted me from behind the counter. There was another customer at the counter, an older woman with a flight bag and a little suitcase. She seemed to be window shopping.

She wasn't ready for the clerk to help her yet, so I asked, "Do you have one-pound boxes of chocolate-covered nuts?"

At that point the customer said, "Sure they do! They've got one-pound boxes of all kinds of nuts!"

I looked back at the clerk, who was, after all, the real authority. She could see that I was waiting for *her* answer. "Yes," she said, "we can make up a one-pound box of all kinds of chocolate-covered nuts."

"Do you have a one-pound box of turtles, chocolate-covered nuts with caramel?" I asked.

The customer again interrupted, "Yes, they have those in one-pound boxes. They also have them in three-pound boxes!"

I looked at the clerk, waiting for the reply from the real

authority (not content with the dubious opinion of just another customer)! The clerk looked nervously at the customer who kept interrupting and finally said, "Yes, we do have them in one-pound boxes. We also have them in three-pound boxes."

At this point the customer again intruded with her unsolicited advice: "But I recommend you take the one-pound Colonial box. It has creams in it, too."

The clerk on the other side of the counter said, "Yes, why don't you try the one with the creams? The Colonial is really a very good box!"

I thought to myself, *Who's working for whom around here?* It really became quite exasperating. "How much is the Colonial box?" I asked.

The clerk told me how much it was, and then the customer added, "Really, their Colonial box has everything. It has chocolate turtles, chocolate-covered nuts, cashews, walnuts, and peanuts. They're beautifully packaged too!" she added. Just then she looked at the clock and said, "Oh, I've got to go or I'll miss my plane!"

Then she picked up her bag and left. Both the clerk and I breathed sighs of relief.

Immediately the clerk turned around and called through the door that led to the back room, "Okay, girls, you can come out now. Fannie Mae is gone!"

"You're kidding!" I gasped.

"I'm not kidding!" she said, "That's Fannie Mae. Well, that's not her real name. When she married her husband, he died and left her the candy stores, so she decided she was going to make something out of her life. She put together some new recipes and packaged some new candies and now has 117 stores all up and down the United States! She calls them her 117 children, and all she does is fly around and visit them all."

Fannie Mae was the authority, but I didn't want to listen to her. She knew all the recipes, she had put the whole thing together, and I was foolishly looking to some clerk as the authority—a clerk who probably never made a chocolate in her entire life!

If you want to know about God, life, prayer, salvation, heaven, or hell, then listen to the real authority. Ministers, theologians, priests, and psychologists at best are clerks. The real authority is Jesus Christ.

What do I know about heaven? What do I know about hell? Am I afraid to die? All I know is that whatever is out there, I am well connected. Jesus has gone ahead of me. He is my Savior. He lived and died on a cross for me. He rose again and He is my friend. I am saved from despair. I have hope! THAT is salvation! And that is what God's love can do for YOU!

Michael McCulloch was an internationally famed psychiatrist, the founder of Delta, the people and pets relationships organization. Sadly, he was brutally murdered.

I talked with his wife, Jane, shortly after I heard the shocking news. When Jane married Michael he was an agnostic. Jane said, "He would have been an atheist, except he was too smart to go that far."

When his fifth child, Molly, was born, Michael suddenly realized that he had spent too many years chasing a career, making more money, and buying bigger houses. One day he looked at Molly and said, "You know, I've missed seeing all the children grow up."

About the same time a physician at the hospital where Michael practiced invited Michael and his wife to his home for dinner. This couple told the McCullochs how they had been dissatisfied with their life, too, and had felt they were chasing false rainbows. They invited Michael and Jane to join them at some Bible studies. Not long thereafter Michael began attending church, and he rapidly embraced faith in the Lord. This faith proved to be his family's salvation as well as his own.

One day, Michael got up early and left while the family was still asleep. He took a swim, went to the chapel, and then made his rounds.

Jane later described a day she will never forget. "My son, Ray, got up and left for his job at a nearby ranch. Amy, Molly, and I were home. I had not been feeling well and was lying in the TV room while Molly watched "Sesame Street.""

I went into the kitchen and turned on a classical record station. Suddenly they interrupted for a news flash: 'A Portland psychiatrist has been murdered in his downtown office.'

"Well, in Portland, many of the offices of the physicians are clustered around the hospitals. When I first heard that, I tried to think of some other psychiatrist who worked downtown. But I couldn't, and I began to get a little nervous. So I decided to call the office and make sure Michael was all right. I called and got the answering service, and that confused me a bit because it was 10:30 A.M. Then I really began to worry.

"I started to question the answering service, and then I just said, 'Never mind.' I called the office back on another number. When I got through to one of the receptionists whom I knew really well, I said, 'This is Jane McCulloch; I'd like to speak with Michael. I just heard someone got shot and I want to see if he's okay.'

"The woman that answered said, 'Just a minute.' She didn't say, 'Michael's all right.' Then she said again, 'Just a minute,' and she put me on hold. By then I had a pretty good idea that it was Michael who had been shot. Then one of Michael's partners got on the phone, and he stuttered and stammered a little bit, and he finally said, 'Uh, Michael's dead.' "

I asked Jane, "How in the world did you get through it?" Listen to her answer:

"Well, we all know that life is a do-it-to-yourself project and it's a multiple choice. And when I got off the telephone, I gave myself a multiple-choice test. We all do this whether we're conscious of it or not. When you go through anything like that you'll say out loud, or you'll say to yourself, 'I can't take this.' Or, 'It's going to be tough, but I'm going to take it.'

"I gave myself that multiple-choice test, and Molly came toddling through the kitchen, and there was no doubt for me what my choice had to be. The only way to go was forward.

"Dr. Schuller," Jane continued, "you know life is like a mosaic. Michael and I had visited St. Peter's in Rome, and we fell in love with the beautiful mosaics we saw there. They're all fitted with stones. And some of the stones are very black, and some of them are very bright. And I think of life as a mosaic. We have a Master Artist, and He puts the pieces in, and in the end it makes a beautiful picture. Sometimes you'll question the Artist and you'll say, 'Why would He put that piece in at that time?' But then I hear the Lord saying to me, 'Jane McCulloch, this is really none of your business. I put that piece in exactly when it was supposed to be put in. You do what you're supposed to do down here, and you let me take care of the eternal things. Don't ask *why*.'"

A memorial fund was established in Michael Mc-Culloch's memory. Through the fund Michael is still giving. Money from that fund was given to the Crystal Cathedral for the purpose of feeding hungry children. At Christmas hundreds of hungry children, in the worst poverty pockets that exist in Southern California, received food in memory of the love of Michael McCulloch.

So his life goes on—over there! And over here, too! It really is possible! Success is never ending! And failure is never final!

Epilogue

Now, my friend, believe me when I tell you that you can make your dreams come true.

The ball is in your court. You and you alone will decide where you will be five, ten, twenty years from today. I've shared all I can with you. Now you have to strive to succeed.

How do you make your dreams come true? You become a Possibility Thinker. You dream a beautiful dream. Where do you get the dream? In positive prayer. Jesus said, "Ask, and it will be given to you; seek, and you will find; knock, and it will be opened to you" (Matt. 7:7). Through prayer the life of God can come into your life! "In Him we live and move and have our being" (Acts 17:28). The Bible correctly analyzes human vitality and energy in that sentence. *"In Him we live."* He gives us a dream, and that gives us life! *"In Him we move"*—ahead! Courageously! Daringly! Now! *"In Him we have our being!"* We discover our true identity—co-workers with Christ on earth!

So get started by moving!!

How do you MOVE?

• Some people shuffle.
• Some people stroll.
• Some people walk fast.
• Some people jog.
• Some people run.
• Some people RACE!

You and your dreams come true if you move with a sense of urgency. The word is S-T-R-I-V-E! At this moment grab hold of that word "strive." Feel the energy this word produces and ease your consciousness with these six letters. Let your positive emotions be charged up with this power producing word—"strive"—and you will arrive!

S — Start Small

T — Think Possibilities

R — Reach a Little Further

I — Invest Wisely

V — Visualize Success

E — Expand Carefully

S: Start Small

Begin with a dream, a prayer, no money at all. That's how dreams come true. You strive, but you start small. You don't jump in wildly and recklessly. Start small; get your feet on the ground; make sure you've got your act together; make sure that you've got control and you know where you're going. Don't start big; you'll choke. Start small. "Inch by inch, anything's a cinch."

Some of you aren't Christians. I invite you now to choose to become a Christian. How? Not by swallowing the whole Bible. Start by accepting the fact that Jesus lived, died, and lives today. If you'll just start to tune into Him, wonderful things will start happening. I'll stake my life, my fortune, my reputation, on this promise! Try it! Now! Here's my invitation to you to become a Christian! You can *choose to forego it—or go for it!*

T: Think Possibilities

"Impossible!" Don't believe in that word! You may have to revise your plans, rearrange your priorities, remodel your blueprint, redesign your strategy, relocate your power center, recheck your traditional answers, get out of the rut, but *it's not impossible.*

You say, "I have a dream, but it's impossible," and I say your dream's not impossible. You just haven't learned how to do it yet. You may have to contact smarter people or find somebody who can invent a new procedure.

You say, "I'd like to move ahead with my dream, but it's not possible, Dr. Schuller." And I reply, you just have to solve some problems, that's all. And that means you may have to make some tough decisions or set new goals.

You say, "I have a dream, but it's impossible. I don't have the money." And I say to you, it's not impossible. All you have to do is collect the money. Increase your income, cut down on your expenses, eliminate waste; but don't tell me it's impossible, because it isn't.

R: Reach a Little Further

Now, stretch your imagination. You can be more than you are. Reach out. Reach for the stars. The farther you stretch yourself, the farther you'll go.

I used to tell my children that if they wanted to get a *B,* they'd better aim for an *A.*

I: Invest Wisely

Now, start putting aside money and energy. Be prepared to put your reputation on the line. But be careful how you spend yourself, your dollars, your emotion, your energy, and your reputation. Watch out who you connect yourself with. Tie up with honorable people. "Where your treasure is; there will your heart be also," Jesus said. So once you've staked your reputation and your possessions on your dream, you'll really be motivated to proceed!

V: Visualize Success

Visualize the dream. I can see my newest dream clearly in my mind's eye. I see a Crystal Cathedral spire with a prayer chapel at the bottom! And I see the bells hanging in there, and I can hear the carillon ringing. I see the people praying! I visualize it very clearly.

E: Expand Carefully

Now, be prepared to enlarge your base. Expand—surely, safely, and successfully. You know, I have accomplished a little, but it took me many years! I will accomplish a lot in the next twelve years! You can't stay where you are; you have to let your success grow or it will begin to die.

So you've made it? You've seen your dreams come true? Then look for a way to expand and grow and keep on dreaming! *"In Him we live and move and have our being."* Make sure that God is in you and that you are in God.

A Closing Prayer

Lord, I want your heart to be in my heart. For in You I come alive, moving ahead from boring death to exciting life!

In Your promises, I will move from discouragement to hope.

In Your pardon, I will move from shame to glory.

In Your power, I will move from weakness to strength.

In Your providence, I will move from failure to success!
Thank You, Lord.
Amen.

NOTES

NOTES

NOTES

NOTES